Thomas Gray

Updated Edition

Twayne's English Authors Series

Bertram H. Davis, Editor

Florida State University

TEAS 6

Frontispiece for "Elegy Written in a Country Church-Yard"

Thomas Gray

Updated Edition

By Morris Golden

Twayne Publishers
A Division of G. K. Hall & Co. • Boston

Thomas Gray, Updated Edition

Morris Golden

Published by Twayne Publishers
A Division of G. K. Hall & Co.
70 Lincoln Street
Boston, Massachusetts 02111

The illustrations are reproduced from *Designs by Mr. R. Bentley, for six poems by Mr. T. Gray* (London, 1753) by permission of the Smith College Library Rare Book Room.

Copyediting supervised by Barbara Sutton
Book production by Gabrielle B. McDonald
Book design by Barbara Anderson

Typeset in 11 pt. Garamond
by Modern Graphics, Inc., Weymouth, Massachusetts

Printed on permanent/durable acid-free paper
and bound in the United States of America

Library of Congress Cataloging-in-Publication Data

Golden, Morris.
Thomas Gray: Updated Edition. / by Morris Golden.
p. cm.—(Twayne's English authors series ; TEAS 6)
Bibliography: p.
Includes index.
ISBN 0–8057–6961–7 (alk. paper)
1. Gray, Thomas, 1716–1771—Criticism and interpretation.
I. Title. II. Series.
PR3504.G57 1988
821′.6—dc19

To Hilda

Contents

About the Author
Preface
Chronology

Chapter One
Gray, the Man 1

Chapter Two
Literary Views 18

Chapter Three
Early Poems 32

Chapter Four
"Elegy Written in a Country Church-Yard" 54

Chapter Five
The Pindaric Odes 69

Chapter Six
Minor Poems 90

Chapter Seven
Classical or Romantic? 115

Notes and References 135
Selected Bibliography 144
Index 152

About the Author

After immigrating from Rumania in 1928 at the age of two, Morris Golden grew up in Brooklyn, served in the U.S Navy in World War II, and in due course received a B.A. from the City College of New York and an M.A. and Ph.D. from New York University. After a career of thirty-five years at New York University, Bowling Green State University, and—for twenty-four of those years—the University of Massachusetts, he retired from teaching in 1986, though he continues to read and write in Amherst, Massachusetts.

Since the mid 1950s, Morris Golden has been trying to catch aspects of eighteenth-century literature and society in a great many articles as well as in *In Search of Stability: The Poetry of William Cowper* (1961), *Richardson's Characters* (1963), *Thomas Gray* (1964), *Fielding's Moral Psychology* (1966), and (with the help of a Guggenheim Fellowship in 1968–69) *The Self Observed: Swift, Johnson, Wordsworth* (1972). For a number of years, Golden has searched the chaos of eighteenth-century English journalism for light on how prominent events and people can have affected the novels of Richardson and Fielding. As his recent work has argued, the forms of political life and the novelists' conceptions of themselves fused to shape their best fiction. Currently, he is attempting to extend this interest in the converging effects of the writer's sense of himself and of the larger pressures of his times to other writers of the eighteenth and nineteenth centuries.

Preface

In the following study, I have had two main aims in view: (1) to give the reader as much information about Thomas Gray, his poetry, and his age as he will need for enjoyment of the poetry; and (2) to examine all the poems freshly as works of literature. This study begins with a chapter on Gray's personality and his view of himself, since this view forms a recurrent theme in the poems. I make liberal use of Gray's letters in this section, since they are spontaneous and generally pleasing expressions of his nature. As a writer for the *Critical Review* said, approving William Mason's reliance on Gray's letters in his biographical *Memoirs* of Gray,

> we may sometimes wish to see a great man in his *robe de chambre,* divested of his pomp and formality; . . . probably an author may appear to more advantage in a negligent habit, than in a full dress; . . . we have the genuine criteria of his genius and virtues in his familiar epistles; . . . we cannot but be pleased with a little native simplicity, and gaiety of heart; and . . . every reader of sense and candor will make allowances for the inaccuracies of an extemporary production. It may be observed, that we are indebted for a great deal of elegant entertainment and historical information to the private letters of Tully, Pliny, Pope, Swift, and other eminent writers; and, that ingenious men, in the warmth of friendship, and the intercourse of a literary correspondence throw out a number of sprightly sentiments and acute remarks, which perhaps would not have entered into their imagination on any other occasion.[1]

The second chapter discusses Gray's theories of literary composition, to which he attempted to adhere in his poetry. Chapters 3 to 5 examine Gray's chief poems in chronological order; chapter 6 deals with incidental pieces, fragments, and posthumously published poems. Chapter 7 attempts to describe the distinctive qualities of neoclassicism and romanticism and to show Gray's position in English literary history in terms of these qualities. While I do not expect to settle the definitions of these complex terms in a brief chapter, I hope that it may provide a reasonably clear introduction to them.

For their kindness in allowing me to use their resources, it is a pleasure to thank the librarians of Bowling Green State University; the University of Michigan; the University of Massachusetts; Smith College; Amherst College; and the Widener and Houghton libraries at Harvard University. I wish to thank Miss Stella J. Sheckter of the New Hampshire State Library for providing me with a typescript of the "Sketch" of Gray that appeared in the *London Magazine*, and Mrs. Richard Haven of the University of Massachusetts Library for locating various materials for me. I am especially grateful to my colleagues, professors Howard O. Brogan and John C. Weston, Jr., for reading several chapters of the manuscript and for providing valuable comments on them. For this second edition, it is a pleasure to thank Virginia E. Garrand and Melinda McIntosh of the University of Massachusetts Library; the staff of the Smith College Library Rare Book Room; Athenaide Dallett, Liz Traynor, Lewis DeSimone, Michael Sims, and Gabrielle B. McDonald of Twayne Publishers; and Professor Bertram H. Davis of Florida State University for their special assistance.

I acknowledge with gratitude the kind permission of the Clarendon Press, publishers of Gray's *Correspondence*, to quote at length from that superb edition. The four reproductions from *Designs by Mr. R. Bentley for six poems by Mr. T. Gray* are by permission of the Smith College Library Rare Book Room, as ever gracious to visiting scholars.

Morris Golden

Amherst, Massachusetts

Chronology

1716 Thomas Gray born on 26 December to Philip Gray, scrivener, and Dorothy Gray, milliner, in Cornhill.

1725-1734 A student at Eton.

1734 Admitted in October to Peterhouse College, Cambridge.

1736 Inherits in February the small property of his aunt, Sarah Gray.

1738 Leaves Cambridge in April without a degree, expecting to study law at the Inner Temple in London.

1739 Begins tour through France and Italy with Horace Walpole on 29 March.

1741 Quarrels with Walpole in May at Reggio, Italy. Returns to London in September. Philip Gray, Gray's father, dies on 6 November.

1742 Richard West, Gray's closest friend, dies on 1 June. Gray returns in October to Peterhouse College, Cambridge, as a Fellow-commoner.

1743 Granted an LL. B. degree in December.

1745 Reconciled with Horace Walpole in November.

1747 Eton ode published in May.

1748 Eton ode, "Ode on the Spring," and "Ode on the Death of a Favourite Cat" published in R. Dodsley's *Collection of Poems* in January.

1749 Mary Antrobus, Gray's aunt and his mother's former partner, dies on 5 November.

1751 "Elegy" published on 15 February.

1753 Gray's mother dies on 11 March. *Six Poems* published in March.

1756 Migrates in March from Peterhouse College, Cambridge, across the street to Pembroke College, Cambridge.

1757 *Odes* ("The Progress of Poesy" and "The Bard") published in August. Rejects offer of poet laureateship in December.

1759 Moves in July to London, where he stays most of the next two years, mainly to read at the British Museum.

1761 Gives up London residence in November. For the remainder of his life he resides at Cambridge, making frequent excursions to London and to other parts of England, as well as to Scotland and Wales.

1768 *Poems* published by Dodsley in March. Appointed Regius Professor of Modern History at Cambridge in July.

1769 "Ode for Music" performed on 1 July at the installation of the duke of Grafton as chancellor of Cambridge University.

1771 Thomas Gray dies on 30 July.

Chapter One
Gray, the Man

In an age that we like to think put a high premium on objectivity, on the distance between the poet and his poem, Thomas Gray was a plausible candidate for greatest living poet, a possible companion to Shakespeare, Milton, and Dryden, after whom he listed himself in "The Progress of Poesy." During the succeeding two centuries Gray has been lowered several steps, partly because of the towering greatness of the poets of the nineteenth century, but perhaps mostly because of the change in critical perspective ushered in by romanticism. We may (as I do) still think him the best poet of his time, but we must admit that the period fascinates by its prose, not its verse or drama. Gray remains, however, on the basis of only three major poems and three or four others—none of them long—within the pantheon of those poets with whom familiarity is inescapable for anyone educated in the English language.

Like Edmund Spenser, whom he immensely admired, Gray was a poet's poet, a grand master of poetic craft in detail and at large; and his work must be the study of anyone attentive to the development of such aspects of English verse as meter, rhyming techniques, musical effects, stanzaic form, and diction. Such technical virtuosity suggests a high degree of detachment from the raw material of experience, an alienation from the concerns of mankind at large. But in at least one of his poemss, the "Elegy Written in a Country Church-yard," mankind has felt itself to be directly addressed by a very sympathetic, human voice. The inconsistency between this effect of the "Elegy" and the apparent aloofness of Gray's other poems (notably his Pindaric Odes) has caused generations of readers to speculate about the connection between the poems and the personality behind them.

In the nineteenth century a favorite critical vulgarization required that the poet be "sincere" in expressing his emotions and that these be violent. Shakespeare's sonnets were read more in the hope of discovering which person they were addressed to—critics being sure there was such a person—than for the sake of responding to the poet's response to complex emotions, no matter what their external stimulus. It is no doubt true that a good poem must deal with something important and basic to the poet; but this does not mean that if he writes about being in love, he must, at the moment of composition, in fact be in love. Rather, his underlying psychological orientation to love must develop itself honestly in the poem. If he can imagine himself into the situation of being a lover and if he communicates that situation so that readers can recognize it as enriching meaning in their world, he has done what he should. From the psychological orientations that recur in a writer's successful work—from the stances that his art effectively projects—we can make inferences about what is congenial to his mind and personality. With the help of those inferences, we can move back into the work and see how their sincere expression has helped give it shape and power.

It would be absurd, for example, to insist that "My Last Duchess" is insincere because Robert Browning never happened to murder his wife out of jealousy and pride. But the effect of the poem shows that he could passionately feel himself into those attitudes, which to a greater or lesser extent we all recognize as being shared by us, and which are essential in Browning's sharing with us his vision of a world. If much of Browning's writing reflected the situation or theme or motive of this poem, however, we could usefully generalize about it as characteristic of his personality. Similarly, we cannot often explain any one poem—for example, the "Elegy"—as a response to any one event in Gray's life. But we can examine all of Gray's poems, together with his other writings, to find to what extent his poetry reflects his own personality. In modern terms, we can search for the image of the self that Gray projected in his poems. To achieve the proper perspective from which to undertake this search—to have a check on the self as it appears in the poems alone—we can examine how Gray appeared to succeeding critics, to his contemporaries, and, most importantly, to himself.

R. W. Ketton-Cremer, Gray's most satisfactory English biographer, tends to see Gray as directly reflecting his experiences in his poetry. An early poem sums up "in a few seemingly artless lines his loneliness, his obscurity, the desolating sense of time passing and nothing achieved which Milton had felt at twenty-three and he himself was feeling at twenty-five." The poems of the summer of

1742, according to Ketton-Cremer, "are clearly linked in thought and mood. The same themes run through all—the flight of youth, the certainty of suffering and death, the inevitability of human fate." Similarly, this critic believes that in the "Elegy" the considerable revision was intended partly to introduce "a fresh note . . . , a sudden note of human loneliness and anguish in the face of death." Furthermore, "At the close of his greatest poem Gray was led to describe, simply and movingly, what sort of man he believed himself to be, how he had fared in his passage through the world, and what he hoped for from eternity." Ketton-Cremer does not, however, attempt to show a personal identification between Gray and the subjects of his famous Pindaric Odes, "The Progress of Poesy" and "The Bard."[1]

The even more perceptive Roger Martin, whose *Essai sur Thomas Gray* is still the best book about Gray, regards him as deeply involved in all of his poetry. Indeed, he sees a close link between it and the extreme psychological difficulties that he thinks beset the poet. Most conspicuously, Martin thinks that "A barrier separated him from the world. He seemed concentrated, enclosed in himself: completely pensive and melancholy."[2] According to Martin, since both of Gray's parents were said to have died of gout (the ailment that tortured Gray through much of his adult life), Gray must have been physically weak, probably arthritic by constitution. Further, he argues that Philip Gray, the poet's father, was at least partly mad, exhibiting qualities of the alcoholic in his moroseness, instability, and domestic violence.[3] Since all eleven of Gray's brothers and sisters died in infancy, Martin concludes that the father had a debilitated nervous system, which his surviving son inherited: the result was that the poet "saw himself as physically inferior," and his symptoms added up to an anxiety neurosis. "A distaste for life, a sense of the nothingness of his existence, impotence to act, these are, in fact, the consequences of this constitutional inferiority."[4]

These are also the consequences that Martin sees reflected everywhere in Gray's poetry. Examining all of Gray's poems, from the Latin stanzas written while he was touring Europe in 1739–41 through the Pindaric Odes of 1757, Martin develops most thoroughly and most extremely the view that Gray's famous seclusion and isolation, his aristocratic aloofness from the mob, form a neurosis that constitutes the basic psychological stuff from which his poetry was drawn. Other recent writers, attempting to assess the personality both of the lonely man and of his poetry, have said much the same thing.

Gray's contemporaries, who had neither the detailed biographical information that is now available, nor effective psychological tools with which to appraise it, thought him very odd, particularly on limited acquaintance. In a reminiscence by the ebullient Lady Phillipina Knight, who had known Gray casually in her youth, we can see him as a rather pathetic figure, self-enclosed against the aristocracy that he both despised and envied:

> I lived some time in a lodging where Gray had apartments. . . . By accident we often met in our landlady's back parlor. He bowed like an undertaker, and I curtsied to him as if I thought him a queer body. My landlady said he was the famous churchyard writer, and I, with a buffoonery natural to me, said that I suppose he is going to make epitaphs for the dead of this parish (St. James's). Hearing he was a Cambridge man, I asked a fellow about him, and he replied: "He is low-born, and no education can make a gentleman of him. His self-sufficiency has smothered his talents in their birth, and his want of temper will render him ridiculous in the place of the world. The most powerful to torment him are his own college, because not only university but universal contempt is the consequence."[5]

Casual acquaintances, who could not have penetrated beneath Gray's aloofness, tended to find him sour or pretentious. Christopher Smart—the poet later famous for his madness, his engaging and warmhearted irresponsibility, and his fine "Song to David" and touching *Jubilate Agno*—was a Fellow at Pembroke College, Cambridge, at a time when Gray, a Fellow at Peterhouse College, had close contact with affairs at Pembroke. Gray was contemptuous of Smart, who had a talent for getting into trouble over drink and debts. Smart, for his part, was both irreverent and perceptive in his impressions of Gray: "Those who remember Mr. Gray when at the University of Cambridge, where he resided the greater part of his life, will recollect that he was a little, prim, fastidious man, distinguished by a short, shuffling step. He commonly held up his gown behind him with one of his hands, at the same time cocking up his chin and perking up his nose."[6]

During his residence at Cambridge, Gray was notorious for his fear of fire, though it was well justified by the frequency of fires in eighteenth-century England. A house belonging to Gray's mother in Cornhill, a number of houses across the street from it, and the residence hall in which Gray lived at Pembroke suffered in various degrees from fires.[7] But though the worry was understandable, it was nonetheless funny to the undergraduates at Peterhouse. A group of them assembled under his windows one midnight, called "Fire," and were rewarded by the sight of his disapproving face framed by a "delicate white night-cap."[8] His summary of the consequence, which was his moving across the street from Peterhouse to Pembroke, conveys his lofty disgust with the hoi polloi: "this may be look'd upon as a sort of AEra in a life so barren of events as mine, yet I shall treat it in Voltaire's manner, & only tell you, that I left my lodgings, because the rooms were noisy, & the People of the house dirty" (*C,* 2:458). As Gray remained longer at Cambridge, and as his fame grew as a poet, his aloofness awed the boys. According to Leslie Stephen, "Gray was so secluded in his Cambridge cloister that the young men made a rush to see him in later years . . . when he appeared by some rare accident in the college walks."[9]

The most embracing eighteenth-century appraisal of Gray—so apt that it has been quoted in most succeeding biographies—was written soon after his death by William Temple, who was a member both of Gray's small circle of friends and of James Boswell's much larger one. According to Temple, in a letter sent to Boswell, recommended by him for insertion in the *London Magazine* and reprinted by Mason and others, Gray

> knew every branch of history, both natural and civil; had read all the original historians of England, France, and Italy; and was a great antiquarian. Criticism, metaphysicks, morals, politicks, made a principal part of his plan of study; voyages and travels of all sorts were his favourite amusement; and he had a fine taste in painting, prints, architecture, and gardening. . . . But he was also a good man, a well-bred man, a man of virtue and humanity. There is no character without some speck, some imperfection; and I think the greatest defect in his was an affectation in delicacy, or rather effeminacy, and a visible fastidiousness, or contempt and disdain of his inferiors in science. He also had in some degree that weakness which disgusted Voltaire so much in Mr. Congreve: though he seemed to value others, chiefly according to the progress they had made in knowledge, yet he could not bear to be considered himself merely as a

man of letters, and though without birth, or fortune, or station, his desire was to be looked upon as a private independent gentleman, who read for his amusement.[10]

Dr. Johnson, though he quoted Temple's eulogy at length in his *Lives of the Poets,* nonetheless let his temperamental revulsion against the semi-monastic life and poetry not primarily directed toward moral and psychological utility permeate his estimate of Gray. In Cambridge, he wrote, Gray "seems to have been very little delighted with academical gratifications: he liked at Cambridge neither the mode of life nor the fashion of study, and lived sullenly on to the time when his attendance on lectures was no longer required."[11] In this work, Johnson is relatively fair to Gray as a man though grotesquely unjust to the poetry. But in private, particularly in one famous conversation recorded by Boswell, he did not force himself to such charity: "He attacked Gray, calling him 'a dull fellow.' BOSWELL. 'I understand he was reserved, and might appear dull in company, but surely he was not dull in poetry.' JOHNSON. 'Sir, he was dull in company, dull in his closet, dull every where. He was dull in a new way, and that made many people think him GREAT.' "[12]

Gray's friends, though they had good reason to admire and even love him, agreed that he was distant with people unless he found in them something to respect intellectually and morally. William Mason, Gray's poetic protégé, long-time friend, and literary executor, says of him that "it was not on account of their knowledge that he valued mankind. He contemned indeed all pretenders to literature, but he did not select his friends from the literary classs, merely because they were literate. To be his friend it was always either necessary that a man should have something better than an improved understanding, or at least that Mr. Gray should believe he had."[13] Norton Nicholls and Horace Walpole, both close friends, also witness to his exclusiveness—as Gray himself does in his letters. There is no question that for those around him Gray was aloof, and that for posterity the aloofness has become legendary.

But while friends, enemies, and indifferent observers can give us a check on the personality that informs Gray's poetry, they cannot define it for us. Only the poet's own characteristic responses to the pressures of life can tell us how and to what extent he thought of himself. Gray's letters show that he thought of himself with both subtlety and persistence. Everywhere in the letters of this ironic observer of his society who spent almost all of his life from the age of eighteen hidden away in Cambridge, first as a student, then as a resident Fellow, and finally, toward the end, as a professor who lived in fear of having to lecture, this self-consciousness recurs. Aside from his learned studies, his own nature and his personality in relation to other people are his main concern in his correspondence. This concern operates, both deliberately and unconsciously, in almost all of his readable poetry; but it is there so intermingled with the classical conception of the poet's isolation that, without evidence from other sources, we might not be sure of its independent pressure.

In a letter written soon after his arrival at Cambridge, Gray amusingly describes himself as dead and in a cemetery (*C,* 1:11–12). His days there, as he writes to his friend Richard West, "go round and round like the blind horse in the mill, only he has the satisfaction of fancying he makes a progress, and gets some ground; my eyes are open enough to see the same dull prospect, and to know that having made four-and-twenty steps more, I shall be just where I was; I may, better than most people, say my life is but a span . . ." (*C,* 1:34). Along with Thomas Ashton and Horace Walpole, Gray and West had formed an exclusive group at Eton, the "Quadruple Alliance," which devoted itself to classical poetry and disdained the obsession with sports of the surrounding barbarians. But despite their relative closeness at Eton, Gray found it hard at this early stage to break his protective distance even with West: "West sup'd with me the night before I came out of town; we both fancied at first, we had a great many things to say to one another; but when it came to the push, I found, I had forgot all I intended to say, & he stood upon Punctilio's and would not speak first, & so we parted . . ." (*C,* 1:55).

One of Gray's special characteristics he diagnosed as a dull melancholy: "Low spirits are my true and faithful companions; they get up with me, go to bed with me, make journeys and returns as I do; nay, and pay visits, and will even affect to be jocose, and force a feeble laugh with me; but most commonly we sit alone together, and are the prettiest insipid company in the world" (*C,* 1:66). Inertia was an ingredient in this melancholy, as he wrote to Walpole: "I have a sort of reluctance to leave this place, unamiable as it may seem; 'tis true Cambridge is very ugly, she is very dirty, & very dull; but I'm like a cabbage, where I'm stuck, I love to grow . . ."

(*C,* 1:82). In youth, before he became the prey of gout and other ailments real and imagined, he worried even about being too healthy: "the goodness of my own Constitution, is in some Sense a Misfortune to me, for as the health of everybody I love seems much more precarious than my own, it is but a melancholy prospect to consider myself as one, that may possibly in some years be left in the World, destitute of the advice or good Wishes of those few friends, that used to care for me, and without a likelihood or even a desire of gaining any new ones" (*C,* 1:115). An element of considerable importance enters here: Gray's affection for and need of a small number of people close to him.

Despite some of these boyish comments, Gray's attitude toward other people was not deranged. He was capable of judging rationally the problems involved in contact with mankind and the benefits accruing from it, as is shown by a letter to West encouraging him to continue his study of the law: "To me there hardly appears to be any medium between a public life and a private one; he who prefers the first, must put himself in a way of being serviceable to the rest of mankind, if he has a mind to be of any consequence among them: Nay, he must not refuse being in a certain degree even dependent upon some men who already are so." He advises West to study law a few hours a day for a year, after which he can change his mind, having learned much and lost nothing. But he cannot help seeing his own uncertainties reflected in those of his friend: "I am sensible there is nothing stronger against what I would persuade you to, than my own practice; which may make you imagine I think not as I speak. Alas! it is not so; but I do not act what I think, and I had rather be the object of your pity, than you should be that of mine . . ." (*C,* 1:169).

Gray had reason to be depressed toward the latter part of his tour of Europe with Walpole. He was twenty-four years old and had accomplished nothing of note; he neither wished to have a public career nor had much chance of one; he faced a relatively poor, lonely, and insignificant life; and the tensions between himself and his rich companion were doubtless growing, in preparation for the famous quarrel in Reggio in early May of 1741. Nonetheless, in a letter of 21 April 1741, he shows a certain equability in describing to West the changes that he sees in himself after two years abroad: Gray now has a "reasonable quantity of dullness, a great deal of silence, and something that rather resembles, than is, thinking; a confused notion of many strange and fine things that have swum before my eyes for some time, a want of love for general society, indeed an inability to it. On the good side you may add a sensibility for what others feel, and indulgence for their faults or weaknessses, a love of truth, a detestation of every thing else. Then you are to deduct a little impertinence, a little laughter, a great deal of pride, and some spirits" (*C,* 1:181–82). After Gray's return to England, a famous passage in his last letter to West, that beautifully illustrates his tendency to introspection and the precision with which he engaged in it, again refers to the depresssion he felt settling on himself: "Mine, you are to know, is a white Melancholy, or rather Leucocholy for the most part; which though it seldom laughs or dances, nor ever amounts to what one calls Joy or Pleasure, yet is a good easy sort of a state, and ça ne laisse que de s'amuser" (*C,* 1:209).

Apparently, Gray was at many stages of his life convinced that a cure for melancholy existed—willpower: "it is sure, we have great power over our own minds, when we chuse to exert it; & tho it be difficult to resist the mechanic impulse & biass of our own temper, it is yet possible . . ." (*C,*2:571). Again, despondence in a retired life can be ameliorated, he writes, by "the power we have, when we will exert it, over our own minds, join'd to a little strength & consolation, nay, a little pride, we catch from those, that seem to love us. . . . I can only tell you, that one, who has far more reason, than you (I hope) will ever have, to look on life with something worse than indifference, is yet no enemy to it, and can look backward on many bitter moments partly with satisfaction & partly with patience, and forward too on a scene not very promising with some hope & some expectations of a better day" (*C,*2:561).

In general, however, Gray's respect for willpower merely made him unhappier, for he thought he did not have enough of it. He bemoans this lack most frequently when he talks of what seems to him the best defense against despair: work. One example of his repeated prescription for happiness carries with it his own sense of not following it: "The receipt is obvious: it is only, Have something to do; but how few can apply it!" (*C,*2:508). He congratulates his friend Richard Hurd on his involvement in writing, "for to be employed is to be happy. This principle of mine, and I am convinced of its truth, has, as usual, no influence on my practice" (*C,*2:520).

Again, he defends his dilettantism, which filled up quantities of notebooks with minutely detailed notes on a vast range of subjects, against the demand that he sensed for more publication: "To think, though to little purpose, has been the chief amusement of my days; and when I would not, or cannot think, I dream. At present I find myself able to write a Catalogue, or to read the Peerage book, or Miller's Gardening Dictionary, and am thankful that there are such employments and such authors in the world. Some people, who hold me cheap for this, are doing perhaps what is not half so well worth while. As to posterity, I may ask, (with some body whom I have forgot) what has it ever done to oblige me?" (*C*,2:565–66).

In a rarer, happier mood, he informed a correspondent of the joyous self-respect that work gave him: "till fourscore-and-ten, whenever the humour takes me, I will write, because I like it; and because I like myself better when I do so. If I do not write much, it is because I cannot" (*C*,3:1018). His ideal of joy through work is best expressed in a famous passage recalling Swift's praise for anyone who can make two blades of grass grow where one grew before: "I am persuaded the whole matter is to have always something going forward. happy they, that can create a rose-tree, or erect a honey-suckle, that can watch the brood of a Hen, or see a fleet of their own ducklings launch into the water! it is with a sentiment of envy I speak it, who never shall have even a thatch'd roof of my own, nor gather a strawberry but in Covent-Garden" (*C*,2:677).

Part of his sense of isolation as it developed was undoubtedly due to a fear that society would hurt him when it could. Even a friend's caution about a poem's prospects could curb his energy, especially when it reenforced his own critical sensitivity. Mason, for example, wrote that he himself had been the cause of Gray's delay in finishing "The Progress of Poesy." Mason had said that he admired the poem, but he also feared it might baffle the ignorant public: "Finding afterwards that he did not proceed in finishing it, I often expostulated with him on the subject; but he always replied, 'No, you have thrown cold water upon it.' "[14] Accused by his friend Chute of writing a sarcastic letter, Gray showed by his response that he was aware of having developed this weapon for use against all of the outside world, including his intimates: "you must attribute it to a sort of kittenish Disposition, that scratches, where it means to caress; however I don't repent neither; if 'tis that has made you write" (*C*,1:204).

Seeing himself thus isolated in a primarily alien world, Gray often complains of the stupidity and dangerous violence of mankind; and he occasionally mentions his need for a few chosen spirits with whom he can safely communicate. Gray's shock at the death of West, which he had suspected when a letter to West was returned unopened, is accompanied by a characteristic expression of anger at the brutality of people in general. His friend's death he sees as the defeat of one of the few sensitive, chosen spirits—as a foreshadowing of his own similar defeat. "The stupid People had put it no Cover," he writes, "nor thought it worth while to write one Line to inform me of the reason, tho' by knowing how to direct, they must imagine I was his friend. I am a fool indeed to be surprizd at meeting with Brutishness or want of Thought among Mankind . . ." (*C,* 1:213).

At about this same time, Gray's prospects of a career led him to comment with wry wit on the same basic subject. Expecting to be among law students at Cambridge, he begs a correspondent to take pity and write often, "when you reflect how cruelly alone I must be in the midst of that Crowd!" (*C,* 1:216). When he was officially qualified for a degree in law, he could not bring himself to take up this socially advantageous but visibly busy career: if he should become a lawyer, "I do not doubt, but some 30 Years hence I shall convince the World & You, that I am a very pretty young Fellow, & may come to shine in a Profession perhaps the noblest in the World, next to Man-Midwifery" (*C,* 1:220).

The busy life offered him no congenial companions, and there were precious few in the contemplative. He felt isolated even in Cambridge, his chosen milieu, though in time he grew to enjoy playing academic politics. His references to Cambridge—from his first arrival there through his settling in as a resident Fellow, a scholar in a community presumably made up of scholars—steadily mix bitterness and wit on the theme of its dullness. He and others there worship "the Power of LAZINESS. you must know she had been pleased to appoint me . . . Grand Picker of Straws, & Push-Pin-Player in ordinary to her Supinity . . ." (*C,* 1:223). During a vacation, it was true, "Cambridge is a delight of a place, now there is nobody in it. I do believe you would like it, if you knew what it was without inhabitants. It is they, I assure you, that get it an ill name and spoil all" (*C,* 2:693). However, he found the university a refuge from increasingly uncongenial turmoil, perhaps because there "no events grow, tho' we preserve those of former days by way of *Hortus Siccus* in our libraries" (*C,* 2:805).

This contempt for Cambridge was an attitude to be shared only with his friends. Against the larger world, he defended the university that he had, after all, chosen for his home. Following a Scottish tour, he was offered an LL.D. by the College of Aberdeen. He wrote the officials that he was honored by the offer, but he excused himself on the ground that he had qualified for that degree at Cambridge and had never bothered to claim it: "judge therefore, whether it will not look like a slight & some sort of contempt, if I receive the same degree from a Sister-University. I certainly would avoid giving any offence to a set of Men, among whom I have pass'd so many easy, & (I may say) happy hours of my life . . ." (*C*, 2:895). Even if Cambridge did not satisfy him, it was always a valuable retreat from the dangers outside.

Gray's need for a circle of admirers became more acute as he grew older, and he found such admirers more readily available after the great success of the "Elegy." He responded to intelligent offers of friendship with warmth and kindliness. Edward Bedingfield, a reader in Scotland, wrote a glowing letter extolling Gray's poetry, and Gray answered eagerly. He wrote that if Bedingfield's praise had come to him when he was younger, it "might have turn'd my head. as it is, I find myself still young enough to taste the sweets of praise (and to like the taste too) yet old enough not to be intoxicated with them. to own the truth, they give me spirits, but I begin to wonder, they should hurt any body's health, when we can so easily dash them with the bitter salutary drop of misery & mortality, that we always carry about us" (*C*, 2:461). He was a kind friend to the young Norton Nicholls, and his eagerness to befriend the engaging young Swiss Charles Victor de Bonstetten is both startling and pathetic. He reached out for sympathetic youth toward the end of his life as if, like his poems, the young men were to link him after his death with the continuing life of the race.[15]

Gray's attitude toward his poetry, and toward his position as a poet, inevitably reflects his response to his friends and to his possible audience, mankind. His Eton College ode, the first of his English poems to appear in print, was published anonymously, and he denied to questioners in Cambridge that he was its author—he wished to tempt the praise of the world, but he feared to risk its condemnation. But when a few years later the world offered to accept him undiscriminatingly, he was frightened. His famous response to the danger that a sensational magazine would publish the "Elegy," a manuscript copy of which the editors had somehow obtained, is shrinking horror. To Walpole, who had been urging its publication, he wrote:

> yesterday I had the Misfortune of receiving a Letter from certain Gentlemen (as their Bookseller expresses it) who have taken the *Magazine of Magazines* into their Hands. they tell me, that an *ingenious* Poem, call'd, *Reflections* in a Country-Churchyard, has been communicated to them, wch they are printing forthwith: that they are inform'd, that the *excellent* Author of it is I by name, & that they beg not only his *Indulgence,* but the *Honor of his Correspondence,* &c: as I am not at all disposed to be either so indulgent, or so correspondent, as they desire; I have but one bad Way left to escape the Honour they would inflict upon me. & therefore am obliged to desire you would make Dodsley print it immediately . . . from your Copy, but without my Name. . . . If you behold the Mag: of Mag: in the Light that I do, you will not refuse to give yourself this Trouble on my Account. . . . (*C,* 1:341–42)

Several years later, Gray wrote Bedingfield that he would have liked to send him a manuscript copy of "The Progress of Poesy," but that he could not trust the mails with it: though only three copies had gone to his friends, he had "been already threaten'd with publication" (*C,*2:462). He wrote Walpole that this poem was "a high Pindarick upon stilts, which one must be a better scholar than [Dodsley] is to understand a line of, and the very best scholars will understand but a little matter here and there" (*C,* 1:364); and this playful prediction was to come closer to fact than Gray found comfortable. When Dodsley proposed using Gray's portrait as a frontispiece to an edition of the six poems that he had completed by early 1753, Gray responded as if he were being asked to dance naked in public: "the thing, as it was, I know will make me ridiculous enough; but to appear in proper Person at the head of my works, consisting of half a dozen Ballads in 30 Pages, would be worse than the Pillory. . . . I am extremely in earnest, & can't bear even the Idea!" (*C,* 1:372). He refused to permit Dodsley to republish "A Long Story" in the 1768 edition of his poems, on the ground that it was none of the public's business; but with that poem removed, he felt obligated to substitute his previously unpublished Norse and Celtic imitations "lest *my works* should be mistaken for the works of a flea, or a pismire," and "with all this I shall be but a shrimp of an author" (*C,*3:1017–18).

Not only did Gray fear ridicule from his public but he also feared an undiscriminating popularity—a reward that his classical reading (particularly his favorite, Plato) had taught him was inevitably tainted. He was utterly contemptuous when, at the death of Colley Cibber, he was offered the appointment as poet laureate. The designation in theory was to go to the greatest living poet; but, since Dryden had been deprived of it after the revolution of 1688, it had notoriously been a political plum awarded to nonentities. The beginning of his answer to his friend Mason, who had been commissioned to sound him out on the subject, reads: "Tho' I very well know the bland emollient saponaceous qualities both of Sack & Silver [the stipend of wine and money that went with the post], yet if any great Man would say to me, 'I make you *Rat-Catcher* to his Majesty with a salary of 300£ a-year and two Butts of the best Malaga; and tho' it has been usual to catch a mouse or two (for form's sake) in publick once a year, yet to You, Sr, we shall not stand upon these things.' I can not say, I should jump at it. nay, if they would drop the very name of the Office, & call me *Sinecure* to the Kg's majesty I should still feel a little awkward, & think every body, I saw, smelt a Rat about me . . ." (*C,* 2:543–44).

But while wishing to separate himself with disdain from the activities of common men—too vulgar and hurly-burly for him, too dangerous, and too impure—Gray nevertheless was keenly interested in their response to him; and he was keenly afraid that he would be taken at his word and left aside. While working on his Odes, he writes, "as to Humanity you know my aversion to it; wch is barbarous & inhuman, but I can not help it. God forgive me" (*C,* 1:420). But of the same poems he says, "my wish & the only reward I ask in writing is to give some little satisfaction to a few Men of sense & character" (*C,* 1:447). Despite his repeated expressions of unconcern for the public success of his *Odes,* Gray asked all his friends to tell him what they had heard about the poems. Though the Greek motto on the title page was "vocal to the Intelligent alone" (*C,*2:797), in Gray's translation, he became quite feverish and ill about the time of the first indications that the public at large found the poems obscure. Evidently, the two odes were his most highly prized attempts to achieve immortality, to impress his concentrated ability upon the intelligent and the many. Fundamentally, he wanted general acceptance of his poetry and resented being thought a coterie poet.

In this response to public misunderstanding, as well as in his envy of the normal life of rearing families and strawberries, Gray's carefully wrought mask is off. Like most poets worth reading, he desired fame. His expressed contempt of public approval represents a defense against disparagement rather than an ascetic rejection of the world. Like the humble dead of his "Elegy," he cast a longing, lingering look behind into the active world that he thought he had forsaken; and he wanted with it to see affection and admiration. According to Mason, Gray had noted for use in his projected didactic poem, "The Alliance of Education and Government," the observation that "One principal characteristic of vice in the present age is the contempt of fame." "Many are the uses of good fame to a generous mind: it extends our existence and example into future ages; continues and propagates virtue, which otherwise would be as short-lived as our fame; and prevents the prevalence of vice in a generation more corrupt even than our own. It is impossible to conquer that natural desire we have of being remembered; even criminal ambition and avarice, the most selfish of all passions, would wish to leave a name behind them."[16] But despite the generally respectful notices his poems received after the "Elegy," and its many imitations, Gray himself was not a dominant figure among his literate contemporaries. A piece in a magazine aimed at fashionable readers, "The Motives for Writing. A Dream," ranked him (in 1761, after the "Elegy" and the Pindaric Odes) eleventh among current writers, behind Edward Young, Samuel Johnson, Thomas Sheridan, John Hawkesworth, David Hume, Mark Akenside, William Mason, Dr. John Armstrong, Thomas Warton, and Richard Glover. And a recent study of names prominent in the consciousness of readers in the 1760s does not find him very conspicuous.[17]

Once, in a despairing moment, Gray wrote Mason implying the yearning for the continuation of life that fame represented to him: "I can not brag of my spirits, my situation, my employments, or my fertility. the days & nights pass, & I am never the nearer to any thing but that one, to wch we are all tending. yet I love People, that leave some traces of their journey behind them, & have strength enough to advise you to do so, while you can" (*C,* 2:579). Gray sincerely placed his reliance on immortality in Christianity, but he also wanted the earthly duration that only poetic fame could furnish him.

Perhaps we can now make some appropriate generalizations about Gray's character—at least as he saw it—and note some of his primary preoccupations. Most conspicuous in everything he wrote is the question of his relations with the rest of mankind. As Roger Martin pointed out, Gray did not have the guarantees of some sort of security that the feelings for family and sexual love provide. From a horrifyingly unstable home, in which his childhood was marked by his father's frequent violence toward his mother and by the regular birth and burial of siblings, and burdened with an apparently delicate constitution, he was placed as an eight-year-old child in Eton. There mass society eagerly rewarded success in violent sports, but the masters and a few chosen friends were deeply interested in classical studies, a pastime in which he found it congenial to excel. At Eton he became habituated to seeking rest and rewards within an intellectual circle, an elite. From his later responses to life, however, it is likely that underneath he felt not fear alone but also wonder and a yearning for the recognition of the rest of mankind—a recognition that, as he saw, the great poets of the past had eventually won from all.

As an adult, Gray continued to have an intense ambition to be the sort of person that he admired: one who would be conspicuous before those capable of judging, and ultimately before mankind at large as well. Since he feared involvements of a sort he could not understand or respond to, the warmest expression of his affection was for his friends; in most of his adult life this was only for friends who acknowledged his intellectual and artistic distinction. As he wrote several times, his inspiration was likely to come at long intervals and to last only briefly, hence his low productivity as a poet. Only the most finished work was good enough to be exhibited for judgment by a world he could not trust, hence the extremely high quality of everything that he allowed to appear.

A prey to melancholy, perhaps through constitution and perhaps through psychological conditioning, Gray needed to be busy and he had to spur himself continually to work. The result was a number of immense scholarly undertakings, none of which he ever completed beyond indicating in his notebook a superlative command over a great variety of subjects.[18] The admiring comment of the great historian Edward Gibbon—that he wished Gray had left scholarship to the scholars, whose lives could more profitably be spent on it than his, and had written more poems like "The Bard"—while it reflects the wish of anyone who can "taste" Gray (Boswell's image), is really beside the point. Without the pedantic notetaking and organizing, Gray would simply have felt worse without composing any more poetry. The great learning, so evident in the techniques and backgrounds of the poetry, was of course from one point of view another defense against the vulgar world, as Martin says. But, on the other hand, it contributes to the individuality of the poetry. And always underneath there is the fearful and yet ambitious soul that wishes to override its fears and to speak to mankind: to speak, like his best contemporaries in fiction and poetry, through the figure of man—necessarily based on reveries about himself—projected across the world in time and space.[19]

Chapter Two
Literary Views

Aesthetics of Literature

Though Gray studied a wide variety of subjects, the only area to which he brought noteworthy ideas is literary theory, particularly where it deals with technique. In most other respects he shared the intellectual outlook of a great many Englishmen of his time. John Locke's ideas, dominant through the century, so impressed Gray that the most ambitious work he undertook, "De Principiis Cogitandi" (Concerning the principles of thinking), was to have been a verse exposition of Locke's epistemology. Like most of his contemporaries, Gray believed in the basic equality of all people at birth (an idea quite important for the "Elegy"); in benevolence as an ideal combination of virtue and mental therapy; and in education as the best guarantor of useful social development (the subject of his fragment "The Alliance of Education and Government"). Like a majority of his contemporaries in England he was a Whig, much concerned with liberty as it was manifested in the English constitution and convinced that other systems, such as the French, were inferior. His two most elaborate poems, the Pindaric Odes, developed among other ideas the proposition that poetry and liberty are close companions—a thesis also of Alexander Pope's *Esssay on Criticism* (1711), James Thomson's *Liberty* (1736), and Oliver Goldsmith's *Traveller* (1764) and *Deserted Village* (1770), and a favorite idea with other contemporaries.

In general, Gray was an orthodox believer in Anglicanism; he despised the deism of Shaftesbury and he warned his young friend Norton Nicholls not to visit the atheist Voltaire.[1] Nevertheless, and again like many conspicuous figures of his time, he relied morally not only on Christianity but also on the teachings of the classical philosophers, particularly Plato and Seneca, both of whom emphasize the absoluteness of virtue and its ultimate residence in the mind of the individual. Gray believed firmly in all of these moral views—

some of them conflicting, if carefully examined—but to none did he contribute new or notable insights.

Similarly, though Gray was to become a brilliant recorder of the details of botany and insect biology,[2] he scorned pure speculation, again reflecting the practical orientation of his century. An early letter to West from Cambridge shows an attitude that was to remain with Gray through his life:

> I have endured lectures daily and hourly since I came last, supported by the hopes of being shortly at full liberty to give myself up to my friends and classical companions, who, poor souls! though I see them fallen into great contempt with most people here, yet I cannot help sticking to them, and out of a spirit of obstinacy (I think) love them the better for it; and indeed, what can I do else? Must I plunge into metaphysics? Alas, I cannot see in the dark; nature has not furnished me with the optics of a cat. Must I pore upon mathematics? Alas, I cannot see in too much light; I am no eagle. It is very possible that two and two make four, but I would not give four farthings to demonstrate this ever so clearly. . . .(*C,* 1:56)

Like his older contemporary Swift (who also despised mathematics and metaphysics), Gray was satisfied to rely on a combination of classical philosophy and Christianity for general truths.

It was to theories of literature and to the details of his craft that Gray gave his most instructive attention. He believed that passion or emotion and inspiration took precedence over cautious adherence to rules, a view in which he echoed the writers of his time. To Gray knowledge of the classics was vital for the poet, not because, as Alexander Pope wrote, to study nature—conceived as the interlocking truths of the physical, social, and psychological worlds—is to study Homer, but because Homer and the others form an essential body of precedent for approaching nature, for shaping it as the artist must. In form, all of Gray's poetry, like much other poetry of his time, is ultimately based on a classical model or derives from a recognizable classical tradition. Writing of precisely Gray's time, W. K. Wimsatt says, "One motif intrinsic to the poetry of the whole century runs with special concentration here—the method, the bondage, and the main freedom of all English neo-classic and pre-romantic poetry—the principle of imitation or free-running parallel. Imitation not only of the full, ancient, and classical models, Homer or Pindar, Horace or Juvenal, but also, increasingly, as the classical models became, or may have seemed to become, used up, imitation of the whole British tradition and especially of the English poets who had already best imitated or paralleled the ancients—Spenser and Milton especially and, though he was still very near, Pope."[3]

Joining some of his contemporaries in a move from both the Miltonic and the Popian classical, Gray also believed that the lyric, devoted exclusively to the high moments of the soul, is the most glorious form of poetry. It followed for him that all the resources of language, including music and visual imagery, are requisite to the finest lyrical poetry; that every stanza, every verse, every phrase, every syllable of a poem needs to be perfectly finished; and that the poem must be unified. He is above all a craftsman, constructing, on the basis of what he himself recognized as a limited fund of power and imagination, unified and beautifully finished work.

In the eighteenth century perhaps more than at other times, the critical argument raged over the relative importance of that element in art that manifested itself in delicacy, order, precision, and formal perfection and that element made up of wonder, awe, exaltation, the irrational that cannot be precisely defined or circumscribed. The former was called "the beautiful" by critics; the latter, "the sublime." The beautiful was essentially that goal of art described by Aristotle, sought by the poets of Rome's Augustan Age, reemphasized in the Renaissance, and staked out in rules by French and English critics of the late seventeenth and early eighteenth centuries. Alexander Pope in his "Essay on Criticism" most elegantly develops the rules for achieving orderly beauty. Jonathan Swift's famous comment on the writers of antiquity, that they like the bee brought forth "sweetness and light," aptly concentrates this aim in a phrase.

Opposing this view of the goal of art as objectively admirable order was the century's developing admiration of "the sublime," which ultimately derived from the writings of the Greek Longinus. Against the "rules," for example, "The urging by Longinus of the psychological and emotional elements in the creation and understanding of art, his assumption that art should transport as well as persuade, and his emphasis upon boldness and grandeur of conception and upon a capacity for the pathetic—that is to say, for the raising of the passions—as all-important and inherent aesthetic gifts, served as something of an authoritative rallying center for the defense of a subjective and emotional taste."[4] The critical homage to the sublime in the Age of Reason was, appropriately, inaugurated by

Nicolas Boileau, the French poet and critic most famous for his devotion to the rules and order; indeed, following him, a number of critics worked out in elaborate detail the rules for this quality,[5] which for effectiveness would seem to depend on a wild *un*ruliness. To this we may add, as I have suggested, Gray's wish to excel prominently. In the aesthetic terms of the day, Gray combines a respect for the classical canons of "beauty" with a yearning for the freedom and power of the "sublime."

Another strain connected with the sublime, and, like it, usually thought of as subverting the exaltation of reason, was the rise of the "Gothic" in art: the expression of a wish to get away from regularity, symmetry, restraint. The term "Gothic," as Samuel Kliger showed in *The Goths in England,* had been used for centuries in both political and religious argument to stand for "humanity, honor, and simplicity" as against "invertebrate Roman urbanism, effeminacy, and luxury."[6] Artistically, the Gothic manifested itself in architecture, where the restoration, and indeed the creation, of ruins became obligatory for noblemen with money to waste; in the craze for Macpherson, a Scot who published poems that he claimed to have taken down from the lips of highland bards who had received them, through oral tradition purely, from the bards of the early Middle Ages; and in the revival of interest in ballads and in Scandinavian and Celtic literatures. Gray was affected by these conflicting influences, and by others as well; as Bertrand Bronson has said, one of his greatest merits as a poet is his knowledge of and discrimination among a wide assortment of traditions.[7]

Gray's artistic orientation, which reflects his temperamental split between the attractions and dangers of immersing himself in life, may be gathered partly from his responses to nature, which, like his contemporaries, he tended to see as a work of art on a grand scale. When, on a summer vacation as a young man, he spent some time with his uncle at Burnham, he found nearby a pleasant wood, with hills, "just such hills as people, who love their Necks as well as I do, may venture to climb, & Crags, that give the eye as much pleasure, as if they were more dangerous . . ." (*C,* 1:47). On his tour with Walpole, Gray registered both awe and appreciation of the Alps, though fear predominated. At the same time, and always after, he found pleasure and safety in smiling order: "The winter was so far advanced, as in great measure to spoil the beauty of the prospect, however, there was still somewhat fine remaining amidst the savageness and horror of the place . . ."(*C,* 1:125). Among the aspects of Turin that he labeled "beauties" were "streets all laid out by the line, regular uniform buildings, fine walks that surround the whole, and in general a good lively clean appearance . . ." (*C,* 1:127).

Gray's double response is most apparent in his description of the climb up the mountain road to the Grande Chartreuse, one of the most famous passages in his letters: "Not a precipice, not a torrent, not a cliff, but is pregnant with religion and poetry. There are certain scenes that would awe an atheist into belief, without the help of other argument. One need not have a very fantastic imagination to see spirits there at noonday: You have Death perpetually before your eyes, only so far removed, as to compose the mind without frighting it" (*C,* 1:128).[8] After danger, however, he is not quite so ready to sacrifice all for aesthetic effect: "Mont Cenis, I confess, carries the permission mountains have of being frightful rather too far; and its horrors were accompanied with too much danger to give one time to reflect upon their beauties" (*C,* 1:129). In a way, this contrast in his attitudes is later echoed in his works, in the contrast between "The Elegy" and "The Bard," which oppose cyclic regularity with stunning shock.

Though mountain horrors evoked ambiguous responses, the peaceful, fruitful plain—less dangerous to himself—pleased him steadily: "The country of Lombardy, hitherto, is one of the most beautiful imaginable; the roads broad, and exactly straight, and on either hand vast plantations of trees, chiefly mulberries and olives, and not a tree without a vine twining about it and spreading among its branches" (*C,* 1:133). He was delighted everywhere both by the regularity and by the evidences of the classical tradition that man had so long been creating. Siena's cathedral, for example, he found "a huge pile of marble, black and white laid alternately, and laboured with a gothic niceness and delicacy in the old-fashioned way" (*C,* 1:144). With Rome he was overwhelmed: "As high as my expectation was raised, I confess, the magnificence of this city infinitely surpasses it. You cannot pass along a street but you have views of some palace, or church, or square, or fountain, the most picturesque and noble one can imagine" (*C,* 1:146). Like his contemporary Laurence Sterne on his sentimental journey through the plains of southern France, Gray delighted in the energy of the throngs of people and the evidences of nature's fertility.

When, in later life, he traveled through the wilder samples of English and Scottish countryside, the ambiguity between his sense of the sublime and his feeling for himself persisted: of Durham, he writes, "I have one of the most beautiful Vales here in England to walk in with prospects that change every ten steps, & open something new wherever I turn me, all rude & romantic, in short the sweetest Spot to break your neck or drown yourself in that ever was beheld" (*C,* 1:379–80). From the Scottish highlands in the summer of 1765, he wrote just as ecstatically, though not so wonderingly, as he had of the Alps as a young man: "in short since I saw the Alps, I have seen nothing sublime till now" (*C,* 2:894); again, "the Lowlands are worth seeing once, but the Mountains are extatic, & ought to be visited in pilgrimage once a year. none but those monstrous creatures of God know how to join so much beauty with so much horror" (*C,* 2:899). In his response to nature, as in his response to man-made art, Gray shows himself appreciative of the ideal of delicate beauty and of the thrill of the sublime.

But where human art does not seek the equivalent of the heights of rugged mountains, he insists as a craftsman that it must follow the basic principles of its craft. He insists on unity, which he sometimes calls harmony, preferring his "Bard" to his "Progress of Poesy" on the ground that the latter has no "Tout-Ensemble" (*C,*2:503–4). On his European tour, he complains that Andrea del Sarto's "Disputation on the Trinity" is badly painted: "from whence he got his great Reputation I know not, Grace & Beauty 'tis certain he was an utter Stranger to; Harmony in the Tout-Ensemble he was ignorant of. . . . "[9] Mason found among Gray's manuscripts a note that sums up this principle as he applied it to poetry: " 'There is . . . a *toute ensemble* of sound, as well as of sense, in poetical composition always necessary to its perfection. What is gone before still dwells upon the ear, and insensibly harmonizes with the present line, as in that succession of fleeting notes which is called Melody.' "[10]

In the search for beauty, Gray demands clarity, finding for example that though Pope's *Dunciad* is on the whole successful, "The Metaphysicians' part is to me the worst; and here and there a few ill-expressed lines, and some hardly intelligible" (*C,* 1:189). Similarly, he was unhappy at the public's demand for clarification of his own *Odes:* "I do not love notes, though you see I had resolved to put two or three. They are signs of weaknesss and obscurity. If a thing cannot be understood without them, it had better be not understood at all" (*C*,2:508). The point, I believe, is that Gray hated "obscurity" in the sense of fuzziness of thought or diction, just as Pope and Johnson did. But in "The Bard' the references to matters of historical fact had to be phrased in an allusive way because they were prophecy, and in a grand way because the conception called for the sublime in diction as well as in situation.

Again within the complex of ideas summed up in "beauty," Gray was certain that in his own period, or at any comparable stage of civilization, a poet without learning and without a reverence for tradition could achieve only the vulgar, the fashionable, the quickly outworn. The Italian artistic entrepreneur and aesthetician Algarotti—with whom Gray had been put in formal correspondence by an Englishman, William Taylor How—wrote Gray about his plans for developing projects uniting all the fine arts. Gray's answer pointed out exactly those dangers that serious writers in our century have complained of in film making: "Poetry (wch, as you allow, must lead the way, & direct the operations of the subordinate Arts) implies at least a liberal education, a degree of literature, & various knowledge, whereas the others (with a few exceptions) are in the hands of Slaves & Mercenaries, I mean, of People without education, who, tho neither destitute of Genius, nor insensible to fame, must yet make gain their principal end, & subject themselves to the prevailing taste of those, whose fortune only distinguishes them from the Multitude" (*C*, 2:811). Learning would constitute for the poet a protection against corruption by mass vulgarity, just as its pursuit had protected Gray at Eton from athletic barbarism.

Gray was, theoretically, on the side of decorum, of propriety, of the suiting of the technique to the subject with the most painstaking care—as my discussion of his views of technique will attempt to show. But here he faced the inevitable problems that had been settled so grossly by the rule-making critics earlier in the century: What if the subject was a wild one? What if society had changed so since the ancients that Aristotle's guides for imitating nature through it were no longer practical? What if an author succeeded in re-creating human "nature" but failed to achieve unity or elegance? In every case where such conflicts existed, Gray decided for flexibility and "nature" and against the rules.

A literary letter, for example, informs his protégé Mason that modern departures from Aristotle's theories of drama are well justified, especially since the chorus has been eliminated: "A greater liberty in the choice of the fable, and the conduct of it, was the necessary consequence of retrenching the Chorus. Love, and tendernesss delight in privacy. The soft effusions of the soul, Mr. Mason, will not bear the presence of a gaping, singing, dancing, moralizing, uninteresting crowd. And not love alone, but every passion is checked and cooled by this fiddling crew" (*C*, 1:358). We are not surprised to find a great writer discarding clichés of form, but the process is nonetheless pleasant to observe. He is here still on the side of propriety and decorum; he retains the spirit of the classical criteria (and of the neoclassical ones as well) while rejecting outworn apparatus. But he insists also that meaningful literature cannot be mechanically composed: "I know not of any writer that has pleased chiefly in proportion to his *regularity*. Other beauties may indeed be heightened and set off by its means, but of itself it hardly pleases at all" (*C*, 1:359). A passage in his friend James Beattie's *Minstrel* called forth an even stronger repudiation of the rules: "This is charming; the thought and the expression. I will not be so hypercritical as to add, but it is *lyrical*, and therefore belongs to a different species of poetry. Rules are but chains, good for little, except when one can break through them; and what is fine gives me so much pleasure, that I never regard what place it is in" (*C*, 3:1169).

What Gray wanted most from poetry, as these passages and others in his writings show, was significant emotional communication. Despite the primarily intellectual and didactic aims of much of the poetry by his immediate predecessors and some contemporaries (Johnson most conspicuously), Gray was not interested in what he called metaphysical speculation in verse. When, on his tour, he began his Latin "De Principiis," he was aware of an inconsistency between his theory and practice, as he notified West: "Poems and Metaphysics (say you, with your spectacles on) are inconsistent things. A metaphysical poem is a contradiction in terms. It is true, but I will go on" (*C*, 1:183). Gray's antipathy to didactic poetry was to become more settled as he grew older,[11] though he made one interesting attempt at lecturing in verse in his "Alliance Between Education and Government." But here, as Mason points out, he was imitating Lucretius, who had made poetry out of Epicurus's system of philosophy. While by temperament and conviction he could not justify didactic art, he tried the form because in antiquity at least one great poem had been achieved through it, and perhaps also because Pope's *Essay on Man* showed the way.

Gray's description of his chosen poetic medium, lyric poetry, indicates that its capacities for the sublime had enticed him to it: "the true Lyric style with all its flights of fancy, ornaments & heightening of expression, & harmony of sound, is in its nature superior to every other style" (*C,* 2:608). The ornaments, the heightening, and the harmony in general fit with the theorizing and, for that matter, with the underlying wishes of his contemporaries. But unlike such writers as Swift, Pope, Goldsmith, Johnson, and Cowper, Gray has a high and unqualified regard for the "flights of fancy," by which he means essentially what later writers have glorified as the imagination. While for him, as for any poet, the imagination still requires control, he does not, like these contemporaries, fear it as a threat to sanity. For attitudes like this, and for attempting to realize them (as in the two Pindaric Odes), Gray has at times been called a precursor of romanticism.

Another, allied reason for his frequent association with the later movement is his championing of all things Gothic, his admiration for the irrational that the eighteenth century thought of as antithetical to the tradition of the classics. When Macpherson initiated the warmest literary argument of the century as to the genuineness of his bardic translations, Gray was acute enough to doubt their authenticity. But unlike Johnson, who famously attacked both their authenticity and their merit, Gray was immensely stimulated by the note of originality, of savage mystery, that he found in them. After Walpole had sent him two of the Ossianic poems, Gray delightedly asked if they were genuine: "I make this enquiry in quality of an antiquary, and am not otherwise concerned about it: for, if I were sure that any one now living in Scotland had written them to divert himself and laugh at the credulity of the world, I would undertake a journey into the Highlands only for the pleasure of seeing him" (*C,* 2:665). "I am gone mad about them," he writes (*C,* 2:679); and though he had received from Macpherson crude letters that seemed dishonest, yet he continued to admire the poems themselves: "I will have them antique, for I never knew a Scotchman of my own time, that could read, much less write, poetry; & such poetry too!" (*C,* 2:690).

As a substitute for "A Long Story" in Dodsley's second edition of his poems (1768), Gray said that he would send him some new material, "imitations of two pieces of old Norwegian poetry, in wch there was a wild spirit, that struck me . . ." (*C*, 3:983). Again, as with Macpherson, Gray was eager to welcome something new into poetry, preferably something that would transcend the social, the ordinary, the precedented—the body of poetry so fully explored by the classics and by the contemporary school of Pope. What Gray wanted, what scholars generally want, limited by routine and reason as they so often are, was an art that could suggest the nobility and the wild passion that he sensed far below the conscious surface of life. One of Gray's comments on Ossian does much to explain his fascination with primitive poetry in general: in this work, one could "see, that Imagination dwelt many hundred years agoe in all her pomp on the cold and barren mountains of Scotland. the truth (I believe) is that without any respect of climates she reigns in all nascent societies of Men, where the necessities of life force every one to think & act much for himself" (*C*, 2:797–98). In the primitive state (but only there), where no social layers dimmed the light of elemental human response, great poetry could be written without learning.

Gray's aesthetic views, aside from his special studies of sound in poetry and his orientation toward extreme and fine finish, are highly characteristic of his period in their conflicting tendencies. Pulled in both major directions, he necessarily offended such conservative enemies as the *Monthly Review*'s John Langhorne, whose entire notice of the 1768 edition of Gray's poems was: "All that we find new in this collection is, The Fatal Sisters, an ode, the Descent of Odin, an ode, and the Triumphs of Owen, a fragment. These turn chiefly on the dark *diableries* of the Gothic times; and if to be mysterious and to be sublime be the same thing, these deep-wrought performances must undoubtedly be deemed so. For our part, we shall for ever regret the departure of Mr. Gray's muse from that elegantly-moral simplicity she assumed in the Country Church-yard."[12] On the one hand, Gray firmly supported what he thought alive in the neoclassical tradition—a wish for regularity, order, clarity, structural unity, good manners, and the propriety involved in suiting the poem and its subject to each other. On the other hand, he was an advocate of a strain that was becoming increasingly important in the mid-eighteenth century: it sought in poetry an escape to the imagination, an unconfined adventure beyond the limits of reason, a direct communication from the passions and imagination of the writer to those of the reader. The conflict within his own temperament between a desire to reach out fearlessly and bravely, and a fear of being hurt if he should do so, is thus also an expression of the temper of a changing era.

Literary Technique

In his discussions of literary technique, Gray is always concerned, as we might expect, with two main requirements that sometimes conflicted: the necessity of unity and the need to communicate intense emotion through the farthest possible extension of the imagination. Much of what he says illuminates his own painstaking practice; in his letter to Mason rejecting modern choruses, for example, Gray's discussion of Shakespeare is notable for its detailed consideration of problems of poetic effectiveness. Shakespeare is

> particularly admirable in his introduction of pure poetry, so as to join it with pure passion, and yet keep close to nature. . . . The greater part of [tragedy] must often be spent in a preparation of these [strong] passions, in a gradual working them up to their height, and must thus pass through a great many cooler scenes and a variety of *nuances,* each of which will admit of a proper degree of poetry, and some the purest poetry. Nay, the boldest metaphors, and even description in its strongest colouring, are the natural expression of some passions, even in their greatest agitation. As to moral reflections, there is sufficient room for them in those cooler scenes that I have mentioned, and they make the greatest ornaments of such parts. . . . (*C,* 1:359).

Gray's admiration is for poetic daring, for flights of imagery. Though he was himself most adept at deriving universal reflections from the subjects of his poems, explicit moralizing is for him merely one among a number of decorative techniques. Some years later, he suggested to Beattie that he develop a plot action at the end of his *Minstrel,* mainly because "it will throw more of action, pathos, and interest into your design, which already abounds in reflection and sentiment. As to description, I have always thought that it made the most graceful ornament of poetry, but never ought to make the subject" (*C,* 3:1140). Thought, even of the most useful sort morally, is no more than one ingredient of the highest poetry. It should never be allowed to distract from the direct communication of emotion, which is achieved through the expression of ideal truths in sensually perceptible terms, through technical ability to paint and sing in verse.

After this emotional and imaginative aim, unity of effect is Gray's great criterion of poetic competence—and one that caused him endless analysis of the details of his craft. His most famous comment on the writing of poetry, in a letter to Mason, leads to a discussion of the problem of unity. Presumably Gray was too polite to inform an inferior that a certain degree of the undefinable was essential before technique could become an issue: "extreme conciseness of expression, yet pure, perspicuous, & musical, is one of the grand beauties of lyric poetry. this I have always aim'd at, & never could attain. the necessity of rhyming is one great obstacle to it: another & perhaps a stronger is that way you have chosen of casting down your first Ideas carelessly & at large, and then clipping them here & there and forming them at leisure. this method after all possible pains will leave behind it in some places a *laxity,* a diffuseness. the frame of a thought (otherwise well invented, well-turned, & well-placed) is often weaken'd by it" (*C,* 2:551–52).

Sensitive to all aspects of writing, Gray was cautious of the effect that a careless original mold might have on the developing thought. According to Mason, Gray's own practice was consistent with this view: Gray's "conceptions, as well as his manner of disposing them, were so singularly exact, that he had seldom occasion to make many, except verbal emendations, after he had first committed his lines to paper. It was never his method to sketch his general design in careless verse, he always finished as he proceeded; this, tho' it made his execution slow, made his compositions more perfect. I think, however, that this method was only calculated to produce such short works as generally employed his poetical pen; and that from pursuing it, he grew tired of his larger designs before he had completed them."[13] Mason's own bent was toward the large and sloppy.

Among Gray's papers dealing with his intended history of English literature are several relatively developed essays that show much of his concern for finish in detail, a concern closely related to his insistence on unity of effect. "Metrum: Observations on English Metre, on the Pseudo-Rhythmus, on Rhyme, and on the Poems of Lydgate" is a good example of Gray's minute, at times pedantic, concern with meter and with such issues as where to put the caesura (the main pause) in a modern line. The alexandrine (a line of six iambic feet) must have the caesura in the middle to sound right, he says, "And this uniformity in the cesura is just the reason why we no longer use them but just to finish a lyric stanza."[14] Further, "the more we attend to the composition of Milton's harmony, the more we shall be sensible how he loved to vary his pauses, his measures, and his feet, which gives that enchanting air of freedom and wildness to his versification, unconfined by any rules but those which his own feeling and the nature of his subject demand" (332–33).

The beginning sentence of another short essay, "The Measures of Verse," indicates how seriously and in what detail Gray undertook his investigations of the history and nature of his craft: "The measures which I find principally in use among our writers are as follow, being in all fifty-nine" (343). This piece is almost exclusively a catalog of the measures and the poems in which they can be discerned. Toward the end, however, Gray comments, sparsely but characteristically, as a practitioner: "Of all these measures, which we may reduce to six, viz. The verse of fourteen, the alexandrine, the deca-syllable, the octo-syllable, the hepta-syllable, and verse of six; none are now used but the third and fourth; except it be interspersedly to vary our composition, and especially in lyric poetry. Our variety too in the rhyme is much circumscribed, never going further than the use of a triplet, and that rarely. As to any license in the feet, it is only permitted in the beginning of a long verse, where we sometimes use a trochee, and the same foot more freely in shorter measures" (359–60). Consciousness of craftsmanship can go no further.

Though meter, rhyme scheme, melody, and picture meant a great deal to Gray in his search for perfect form, as a craftsman he was at least as much interested in his ultimate tools, words. His diction was even in his own time seen as his peculiar characteristic, as the idiosyncrasy in his poetry for which he could be praised or damned. During the spring of 1742, when Gray was entering his first great period of poetic activity, he wrote to Richard West the pronouncement on diction which was most to be condemned by romantics and postromantics: "The language of the age is never the language of poetry; except among the French, whose verse, where the thought or image does not support it, differs in nothing from prose. Our poetry, on the contrary, has a language peculiar to itself; to which almost everyone, that has written, has added something by enriching it with foreign idioms and derivatives . . ." (*C,* 1:192). The result of this analysis is the diction that Johnson thought monstrous and that Wordsworth chose to show the misguided practices of his predecessors. Gray's word choice is, however, quite defensible, as will be seen in the more detailed discussions of the poems in succeeding chapters.

On language in general, Gray's view is that, to maintain the purity of a lofty emotion, one must avoid colloquial blemishes. To range farthest in the imagination one must range farthest in diction, hence the "gales redolent of joy and youth," to which Johnson objected as beyond the limits of the English language. To reach the widest response in the sensitive reader, one needs to use phrases that will draw on his responses to other poems, hence the frequency of borrowing. And to project poetry's ultimate aim, the ideal, which will arouse the purest emotions, one wishes to use the richest, most sublime language, hence the many personifications.[15] The result is no doubt "artificial," not Wordsworth's language of ordinary men, but then ordinary men do not speak the ideal in the ordinary course of their lives.

Chapter Three
Early Poems

Upon his return from the Continental tour, Gray experienced his single most concentrated period of poetic inspiration. This inspiration was derived from pondering his own place among mankind, and it was much affected by his prolonged and intense subjection to the influences of classical landscapes and Continental culture. Contemplating his situation with respect to others produced little joy; for Gray was now twenty-five and, though conscious of unusual abilities, he was even more aware that he had done little to demonstrate them. He had no professional prospects, no ambitions to practice the law or to take a degree of any sort; he did not wish to make himself a public servant or to deal in any way with the public; he had enough income to live on. His father died that fall, and though there seems to have been no intimacy between them, they had kept up enough cordiality for a correspondence during the tour. Aside from his close ties with his mother, Gray had no expectations of familial intimacy; the one reference in his *Correspondence* to possible heterosexual love (to Walpole, 23 February 1738) seems to dismiss it as a forlorn dream. He must even have had considerable doubt about the natures of the chosen few whose praise he wanted: Horace Walpole, as cultivated as himself and his closest friend, had broken with him and given way to the glittering lures of the world. Their quarrel was so sharp that for years they did not communicate; and even after their reconciliation, their relations, while cordial, were not intimate.

The uncertainties oppressing Gray had been ripening during the trip, and they infused his Latin poetry with the personal quality that competent judges have admired in it. The Latin poems, as various scholars have remarked, exhibit (though with less complexity) the themes with which Gray was to be so preoccupied in the English poems. *"Ad C: Favonium Aristium,"* for example, shows how much better it is to wander among rivers, trees, and valleys than to worship the idols of the crowd; and it develops toward the end the view that Gray wants a quiet, peaceful, isolated life. In Gray's most admired Latin poem, an "Alcaic Ode" written at the monastery of the Grande Chartreuse, he begs the great god of nature to "grant to a youth already weary calm and peaceful rest. But if Fortune now forbids me to enjoy this enviable dwelling and the sacred rule of silence, despite my wish, sucking me back with violence into the midst of the waves, at least, Father, grant that I may spend the hours of my old age free of care in some secluded corner; carry me off in safety from the tumult of the mob and the anxieties of men."[1] In general, whether or not we agree with Roger Martin that the Latin poetry shows Gray's wish to be "assimilated to things" in the mystic pantheism that I for one do not see in him, Gray certainly dreams of leaving the uncongenial violence and clutter of life. While such an attitude undoubtedly echoes both the classical literary tradition and one strain of eighteenth-century wishful thinking, it just as certainly reflects Gray's own temperamental rejection of the stress that life among people inevitably entails.

On his return to England, he would have found the "tumult of the mob" at its height, for the election that was to test the long-term power of his friend Walpole's father as prime minister had just concluded, and everyone was waiting for the new Parliament to discover what it wanted to do. In February 1742 Sir Robert Walpole was indeed toppled, and the following months resounded with bitter divisions and recriminations, all in the context of a dreary war with Spain. There was no lack of object lessons in spectacular futility for anyone looking from a position of even temporary detachment, as witness Pope's contemporaneous *New Dunciad* (1742) and Fielding's *Joseph Andrews* (1742) and *Jonathan Wild* (1743).

In the spring and summer of 1742, Gray turned to English under these stimuli and wrote four completed poems, an extraordinary burst of productivity for him. The first, "Noontide," which was later renamed "Ode on the Spring," he finished in May and sent to Richard West. The letter containing it was returned to him unopened. His own fears, supported by his knowledge of West's illness, led him to infer—correctly—that his closest remaining friend since the rupture with Walpole was dead. To Gray's vague sense of distance from life, and to his accumulated fears about life's shortness deriving from his childhood, was now added the immediate shock of knowing that this intimate friend, talented in the same way as he himself and his twin in sensibility and predilections, had died suddenly before he had accomplished anything of significance.

The result was an added spur to utter as honestly and richly as he could the universal truths about the shortness of life and the inevitability of sorrow, truths that animate the Eton College ode and the "Ode to Adversity" and that combine with the expression of his personal sorrow in his sonnet about West's death. As R. W. Ketton-Cremer has said, "The same themes run through all—the flight of youth, the certainty of suffering and death, the inevitability of human fate."[2]

Three of the four poems completed in 1742 are odes, a form highly popular in the eighteenth century. The writing of odes was practiced in England, according to George N. Shuster, in three main ways: "poems written in uniform stanzas, each of which comprises lines varying in length originally (with Jonson and the earlier poets) but tending toward regularity in later practice (for example, Collins and Keats); poems written in the irregular stanzas brought into vogue by Cowley, and sometimes called *verses irreguliers;* and poems written in the tripartite arrangement of Pindar's heroic odes, with strophes, antistrophes, and epodes. . . . "[3] As any reader can easily see, these early poems of Gray were in the first form; and their manner derives, on the whole, from the cool, controlled emphasis on technique of the Latin poet Horace.

"Ode on the Spring" ("Noontide: an Ode")

Mason, Gray's first editor, says of the "Ode on the Spring":

> The original manuscript title, which Mr. Gray gave to this Ode, was Noontide; probably he then meant to write two more, descriptive of Morning and Evening. His unfinished Ode ["Ode on the Pleasure Arising from Vicissitude"] . . . opens with a fine description of the former; and his Elegy with as beautiful a picture of the latter, which perhaps he might, at that time, have meditated upon for the exordium of an Ode; but this is only conjecture. It may, however, be remarked, that these three capital descriptions abound with ideas which affect the ear more than the eye; and therefore go beyond the powers of picturesque imitation.[4]

Johnson dismisses the poem: "His *Ode on Spring* has something poetical, both in the language and the thought; but the language is too luxuriant, and the thoughts have nothing new. There has of late arisen a practice of giving to adjectives, derived from substantives, the termination of participles, such as the *cultured* plain, the *daisied* bank; but I was sorry to see, in the lines of a scholar like Gray, 'the *honied* Spring.' The morality is natural, but too stale; the conclusion is pretty."[5] Roger Martin, after deducting the triteness of subject and the immense number of literary influences, concludes that the poem is saved by Gray's craftsmanship and, even more, by its psychological honesty.[6]

As various critics have noted, the "Ode on the Spring" is made up of such great numbers of borrowed phrases, of allusions and imitations, that it is hard to find any one line completely original with its author.[7] Furthermore, the poet reclining under a tree preferring nature's hum to man's comes right out of the Latin tradition of the sensitive *poeta.* Nonetheless, as Martin says, the situation is completely honest, for the tradition merely complemented Gray's predilections.

After directing us to the season, the time of day, and the poet's proper vantage point, the poem focuses on a dialogue between the poet and mankind, notably mankind of his own age—"The insect youth" who are "on the wing." The issue between them is how to spend the short mortal life allotted to man, and it is not resolved; it never was for Gray. The connotations of "insect youth" and the direct statement of the fourth stanza—that activity, whether pleasure or business, leads to misfortune, impotent age, and eventually death—seem to favor the life of aloof contemplation. But the concluding stanza makes the life of the retired youth, "A solitary fly," no more attractive: he has no "glittering female," no well-stocked home, and no achievements that adorn him. He has lived to as little effect as they, despite the companionship of his Muse.

The irony underlying the inevitability and permanence of death, no matter how man's life is spent (an irony that Gray could not dispose of to his own satisfaction until the "Elegy," where he sees that solace is to be found in the cyclic return and immortality of the species), is supported both by the diction and by the careful, exactly symmetrical structure that Gray was to develop in all of his completed poems. This ode is fifty lines long, and in line 25 the "insect youth" appear as a contrast to the poet and as preparation for the opposed positions of the fourth and fifth stanzas. Furthermore, the rich coloring, which Johnson objected to and others have found too elaborate to be genuine, is directly related to the ironic point. When was an English spring so lush as to be called "the purple year"? Why should a nightingale in England be described as an "Attic warbler"? Critics complain that this scene is Greek and therefore dishonestly derived from books rather than observable nature. But Gray did not share their assumption that he had contracted to deliver an exact description of an English landscape.

Instead, he contrasts here, as in much of his other poetry, *ideas* in terms of sounds and pictures and the connotations of language. He needs an ideal fecundity of nature, a nature that is rich, colorful, harmonious, sweetly odorous, to balance against the frantic triviality of man attempting to make more of life than, say, insects or flowers can make. Observing this balanced picture is his ideal self, musing on the apparent contrast, not yet having decided what choice he shall take or indeed whether there is a choice—a situation, according to Cleanth Brooks, that gives form to the "Elegy" (and the "Elegy," ultimately at the core of Gray's work, retrospectively answers the "Ode on the Spring"). Nature is an ideal conception here, neither English nor Greek, nor any other place but Gray's mind and the minds of his readers, the residences suitable for "Contemplation's sober eye" and for the insect youth and the solitary fly.

Already, in developing a technique for making the ideal appeal to the senses, Gray sees his art as including a synthesis of the two other most conspicuous arts: music and painting. Particularly, he shows his concern for melody and for what Oliver Elton has called "the full open vowels of the more harmonious language," Latin.[8] Note, for example, Gray's concentration in the first stanza on long, liquid sounds and on the succession of colorful visual images against which man's pettishness is contrasted:

> Lo! Where the rosy-bosom'd Hours,
> Fair VENUS' train appear,
> Disclose the long-expecting flowers,
> And wake the purple year!
> The Attic warbler pours her throat,
> Responsive to the cuckow's note,
> The untaught harmony of spring:
> While whisp'ring pleasure as they fly,
> Cool Zephyrs thro' the clear blue sky
> Their gather'd fragrance fling.

Man has his place in the color and harmony along with the insects, the reflective poet implies, but he wonders whether there is something else for man to be and do. The last stanza only enriches the ambiguities he has posed.

> Methinks I hear in accents low
> The sportive kind reply:
> Poor moralist! and what art thou?
> A solitary fly!
> Thy Joys no glittering female meets,
> No hive hast thou of hoarded sweets,
> No painted plumage to display:
> On hasty wings thy youth is flown;
> Thy sun is set, thy spring is gone—
> We frolick, while 'tis May.

The "Ode on the Spring" is certainly not a major work, perhaps because the mockery both of himself and of mankind generally may seem to echo the sort of thing that Gray had previously done in Latin as college exercises. That is, this ode has the air of being on a set debating theme, "whether it be better to observe life or engage in it." But the poem has a remarkable finish both in structure and in detail, and it indicates a complete readiness with the poet's tools, should a more profound impetus inspire him. That impetus seems to have been West's death, which changed a vague melancholy to an intense involvement in human mortality.

"Sonnet on the Death of Richard West"

Though the sonnet on West was not published until after Gray's death, I consider it in this place because its subject marked the turn in Gray's life that led to the other poems of 1742 and also affected his thoughts and feelings so long as he lived. More than any other of Gray's poems, therefore, it can be used as a document to indicate how the poet dealt with his private feelings and events when making art of them.

Wordsworth chose the sonnet on the death of West as the horrible example of what was wrong not only with Gray but generally with neoclassical poetry, against which, as the self-conscious inaugurator of a new mode, Wordsworth was rebelling:

> I will here adduce a short composition of Gray, who was at the head of those who, by their reasonings, have attempted to widen the space of

separation betwixt Prose and Metrical composition, and was more than any other man curiously elaborate in the structure of his own poetic diction. [Wordsworth quotes the sonnet, italicizing lines 6–8 and 13–14.] It will easily be perceived that the only part of this Sonnet which is of any value is the lines printed in Italics; it is equally obvious, that, except in the rhyme and in the use of the single word "fruitless" for fruitlessly, which is so far a defect, the language of these lines does in no respect differ from that of prose.[9]

Whether or not one agrees with Wordsworth—and readers have differed in their responses to the sonnet—his charge demands discussion since it focuses on Gray's views of his proper relation to his art. Wordsworth is saying essentially that much of the sonnet is emotionally uncommunicative: Gray did not utter the cry directly from his heart, but instead elaborated it in invented, artificial diction. A modern critic makes the same point more directly: "Characteristically, Gray wrote in English a stilted sonnet on West's death and put his genuine feelings into the Latin verses that he appended to his philosophical fragment, *De principiis cogitandi.*"[10] Allowing for the personal preference involved in the choice of words, this remark is perfectly true. In the Latin poem, Gray speaks directly to West, bewails his sudden death and the consequent disappearance from the earth of his virtues, bewails his own loss, and speaks of how he is driven to waste his life because of unsatisfied longing for his friend. The English poem, however, is deliberately framed in the sort of "elevated" diction that places the poet at some remove from his material. To complicate the matter, Gray's ideas may well have been evoked by recollections of a poem, "Ad Amicos," that West had sent him in 1737, predicting that his friends would pay no attention to his death and hoping that his friends would remember him. Some critics have therefore argued that Gray's sonnet is indeed a personal poem, a private response to West's.[11]

Since the issues involved are so basic to an understanding of Gray's poetic aims and techniques, let us look at the complete sonnet:

In vain to me the smileing Mornings shine,
  And redning Phoebus lifts his golden Fire:
The Birds in vain their amorous Descant joyn;
  Or chearful Fields resume their green Attire:
These Ears, alas! for other Notes repine,
  A different Object do these Eyes require.

My lonely Anguish melts no Heart, but mine;
And in my Breast the imperfect Joys expire.
Yet Morning smiles the busy Race to chear,
And new-born Pleasure brings to happier Men:
The Fields to all their wonted Tribute bear:
To warm their little Loves the Birds complain:
I fruitless mourn to him, that cannot hear,
And weep the more, because I weep in vain.

As I read the poem, Gray is again seeing his subjects—himself and West—ideally, as representatives of the dead young man and his bereft friend who are to stand for all young men who die with their promise unfulfilled and for all those who mourn them. The passage in the Latin poem thus becomes a rough sketch, the direct expression of an individual shock. From Gray's point of view, it is the private raw material of poetry—perhaps powerful, but not widely meaningful. That is, even without writing to the public, Gray consciously uses a conventional art form to express the universalized response that is to embrace all of humanity, not his single private and therefore insignificant bereavement. Even if we accept this view, so irritating to some romantics and most modernists, we may still complain with justice that universalizing does not necessarily require the standard phrases, some of which Wordsworth objected to because of their difference from prose, while others might be condemned for triteness: smiling mornings, reddening Phoebus, green attire, the busy race. Though we can see why the clichés were used, I fear that we cannot really excuse them.

So much for the concessions. As for the virtues of the poem, the poet Gerard Manley Hopkins, certainly a competent judge, wrote to his friend Richard Watson Dixon that this sonnet has considerable "rhythmical beauty, due partly to the accent being rather trochaic than iambic. Wordsworth says somewhere of it that it is 'evident' the only valuable part of it is (I believe) 'For other notes' and the quatrain that follows. Such a criticism is rude at best, since in a work of art having so strong a unity as a sonnet one part which singly is less beautiful than another part may be as necessary to the whole effect, like the plain shaft in a column and so on. But besides what he calls evident is not so, nor true."[12]

Aside from the carefully designed melody and the pictures, the pattern of rhyme—which for all conscious poetry is one clear index of the degree of deliberateness of the artist—shows how Gray was concentrating on solving the problems of freshly uniting the sonnet. Both traditional English sonnet forms present problems. The Shakespearean form (*abab, cdcd, efef, gg*) tends to split the idea into three separate though parallel poems, which the closing couplet attempts to unite. The Petrarchan (*abba, abba, cde, cde*) faces the danger of becoming two poems, an eight-line proposition and a response of six. The masters of the sonnet—among whom are Spenser, Shakespeare, Sidney, Milton, Wordsworth, and Keats—built their poems with a full awareness of these inherent difficulties and turned them to advantage. So also did Gray in his only extant attempt. The first eight lines are in the form of two quatrains of alternate rhyme, *abababab,* while the last six are *cdcdcd;* he is, therefore, combining the two forms, leaning perhaps in structure to the Petrarchan contrast of the octave with the sestet. To overcome this possible separation, however, the thought tends to work in the Shakespearian unit of the quatrain. More important as a technical innovation, the rhymes of the last six lines are only slightly different from those of the first eight—that is, "chear" and "expire," "vain" and "mine" are half-rhymes in themselves. Consequently, the poem is so constructed that it is to be seen only as a unit, not as two poems or three and a tail. The identical phrase opening and closing the sonnet is again evidence of the care that Gray took so that a single, though complex, effect would ensue.

A little more may be observed about the construction of this beautifully unified work. It contains three sentences: an opening one of six lines, the gist of which is that the speaker finds no joy in the richness of sight and sound that nature offers and seeks other sights and sounds; one of two lines, pointing out that he alone is affected by this particular sadness, and for him—note the peculiar exactness of Gray's diction—"the imperfect Joys" die undeveloped; and one of six lines showing that the richness of nature is fruitful and fertile, while the speaker spends himself in sterile unhappiness, all the more unhappy because he knows it to be sterile. Without giving up the effect of an intellectually complex and therefore arresting ending, he achieves his usual superb symmetry, with the poem opening out around its center, either of the surrounding parts reflecting on the other and on that center.

The sonnet on West, on the whole, does suffer from occasional triteness of phrasing, a triteness that under another name—literary allusion—was forgivable in its time. But we may well feel that the restraint, the exactness, the richness, the sensitivity, and the formal perfection atone for the fault. As Gosse wrote, there is no sonnet to touch it between Milton and the great romantics. It is not, like the "Ode on the Spring," the product of an artist who has learned his craft but does not have the experience with which to exploit all of his resources. The poetic statement is as complex and ambitious as a mature impetus and a developing technique could make it.

"Ode to Adversity"

More than the "Ode on the Spring," Gray's "Ode to Adversity" fits into the category of the "Great Ode," as a lyric poem aiming at the sublime was called in eighteenth-century England. In it, Gray combines the Horatian qualities of regularity and elegance with the sort of subject (much affected by his contemporary William Collins in a variety of poems, notably "Ode to Fear") in which English ode writers were likely to wax irregular. Though the "Ode to Adversity" does not exhibit the metrical liberty and boldness or the transported rapture that Norman Maclean says were encouraged in that form (qualities more notable in Gray's later "Bard"), it does follow a contemporary pattern in other ways. According to Maclean, the "allegorical ode," a newly popular form in the mid-eighteenth century, is a development of the traditional, and classical, "panegyrical ode" (ode of praise), now addressed to an abstraction. Such poems, he says "are designed ultimately to display not so much the power of the subject addressed as the power of the poet's imagination."[13] It thus was a form appropriate both to Gray's underlying wishes and to his theory of the function of poetry.

The "Ode to Adversity," which to a modern reader may well be the chilliest poem written by Gray, is the only one aside from the "Elegy" that Johnson praises: "Of the *Ode on Adversity* the hint was at first taken from 'O Diva, gratum quae regis Antium' [Horace, *Odes,* 1.35]; but Gray has excelled his original by the variety of his sentiments and by their moral application. Of this piece, at once poetical and rational, I will not by slight objections violate the dignity."[14]

The general thesis of the "Ode to Adversity" is relatively simple, perhaps the reason that Johnson found it so appealing: God has provided Adversity, the "Tamer of the human breast," to teach us to understand the sorrows of others. *Complete Poems* notes some speculation about which daughter of Jove this is: Ate (Blind Folly), Athena, or merely a general female personification derived from Jove. We can rule out Athena, for Walpole's "Explanation" of Bentley's handsome frontispiece for the poem describes Minerva (Athena) and Adversity as different female figures in it. Nor does the respectable matronly Adversity look much like an Ate.[15] Gray admired Bentley's illustrations and interested himself in this edition, so that we can infer Bentley's awareness of his intentions. To return to the poem: Adversity is seen as a leveler of classes (first stanza), just as death appears contemporaneously in the "Ode on the Spring" and later in the "Elegy." But the development of this thesis involves Gray in a complex theme persistent through his work: the union of mankind in the face of certain hardships, the implied union of himself with all, and his simultaneous attempt to distinguish himself from the crowd in the way that he faces the hardship. In this ode, for example, while suffering with the rest, he wishes to do so virtuously. In the conclusion, which Johnson admired and to which even Wordsworth would have had no objections, Gray wishes to have the milder choice: understanding oneself. Roger Lonsdale sees this moral stance as an advance on the Eton College Ode and therefore concludes that the "Ode to Adversity" is the later of the two (*P*, 69); but this is to turn Gray's vision of life into a series of quiz questions and answers. The conditions and themes, however, recur—as they must for a living mind—seeking fresh resolution in every effective poem.

Most of the "Ode to Adversity" is less direct than the last stanza; and, while it is not completely accurate to say—as critics have said from time to time—that Gray is at his best when he is simplest in diction (the "Elegy" is as ornate as anything that he ever wrote), it is true that, in such a poem as the "Ode to Adversity," his point seems strangled in personified abstractions. As Earl R. Wasserman has argued, to Gray's contemporaries the personification was intended to be poetry stretched to the ultimate imagination; and certainly in the next-to-last stanza (lines 33–40) Gray is aiming at the peak of the sublime:

> Oh, gently on thy Suppliant's head,
> Dread Goddess, lay thy chast'ning hand!
> Not in thy Gorgon terrors clad,
> Nor circled with the vengeful Band

(As by the Impious thou art seen)
With thund'ring voice, and threat'ning mien,
With screaming Horror's funeral cry,
Despair, and fell Disease, and ghastly Poverty.

But we are not required to share an outworn taste, and when Gray packs in Wisdom, Melancholy, Charity, Justice, and Pity, with accompanying attributes, in one eight-line stanza, we may feel as Coleridge did about another poem by Gray: "it depended wholly on the compositor's putting, or not putting, a *small Capital,* . . . whether the words should be personifications, or mere abstractions."[16] That is, Gray's personifications in this poem are mechanical, not imagined pictures but only abstract ideas. In contrast to this ode, the attributes of the personifications in the Eton College ode and the "Elegy" are chosen with a sure sense of vividness, precision, and emotional suggestiveness.

As always with Gray, the versification is worthy of special notice. He never repeats himself exactly in any two poems, making of every one an experiment. In the "Ode" he uses an eight-line stanza, in a basic tetrameter with trochaic effects that echo Milton's immensely influential companion pieces "L'Allegro" and "Il Penseroso." Gray opens with four lines of alternating rhyme, follows them with a couplet, and concludes with a couplet the last line of which is an alexandrine. The effect of this last, as always when it is well used, is to emphasize the unity of the stanza that it completes. The change in rhyme and consequently of musical pattern in the middle of the stanza gives the stanza the effect of statement and response.

Again as usual, the poem is symmetrically built around its middle. The first three stanzas present the fiction and the attitude of the crowd. Adversity is divine, the nurse of virtue; "Self-pleasing Folly's idle brood," the offspring of mindless, selfish routine, run away from her manifestations. As a contrast and response to this picture, the last three stanzas present the chosen few, of whom the poet hopes to be one: when affected by Adversity's milder aspect, they can benefit from the virtue that she teaches. The final alexandrine sums up the wish of the poem; it adds the reflective coda, and it responds specifically to the last stanza of the first part, stanza 3. Significantly, the positive side of Adversity at the end is to act on the single poet; the negative has frightened off Folly's idle brood, the mob, in stanza 3. Overall, though the "Ode to Adversity" does not look like a masterpiece from the perspective of the twentieth century, it deserves our respect for its good manners, basic honesty, and structural finish.

"Ode on a Distant Prospect of Eton College"

For most readers the Eton College ode has been the favorite of those poems written in 1742, though some have preferred the perfect unity of the sonnet about West. Johnson, true to form, despised the Eton ode:

> The *Prospect of Eton College* suggests nothing to Gray which every beholder does not equally think and feel. His supplication to father Thames, to tell him who drives the hoop or tosses the ball, is useless and puerile. Father Thames has no better means of knowing than himself. His epithet "buxom health" is not elegant; he seems not to understand the word. Gray thought his language more poetical as it was more remote from common use: finding in Dryden "honey redolent of Spring," an expression that reaches the utmost limits of our language, Gray drove it a little more beyond common apprehension, by making "gales" to be "redolent of joy and youth."[17]

Oliver Elton, writing for most critics with more sensitivity and with fewer axes to grind than Johnson, emphasizes the impressiveness of Gray's poetic technique in the service of an admittedly old idea. Gray, according to him, "arranges his theme like a tragedy," beginning in bright sunshine and leading to a terrible end: "The overture is a mixture of his most natural and tender writing with what seems a painful dose of 'poetic diction'; but the 'idle progeny' and the 'rolling circle's speed' should be read as playful not as pedantic phrases. Then come the foreboded horrors . . . . the pageant of Infamy, Falsehood, Unkindness, and Remorse reminds us, in its power and concentration, of Spenser."[18]

The general theme of the poem, as critics have pointed out, is the same as that of the others of 1742—the inevitability of suffering and death for mankind; but the effect is more tender. In the Eton College ode, for example, Gray is not balancing foolish or vicious expense of life with lonely reflection, as in the "Ode on the Spring." The children who are observed are playing; and play is all that we can expect of them. Therefore, the poet's paternal superiority in knowing their fates while they are ignorant of them strikes us as natural in an adult, not as arrogant. Therefore, also, his preferred symbolic situation—the poet standing aloof in time and place and surveying other people's busy activities, wiser than they are and sadder—becomes perfectly fused with the subject. To put it another way, Gray's underlying sense of superiority to the crowd seems most mature and legitimate when there is a clear, objective justification for it. And since this is not a crowd that he need fear—like the people of his letters, Latin poems, and "Ode on the Spring"—the poem exhibits no self-pity to weaken the dignity. It identifies the poet with mankind (cf. lines 13–14 and the concluding section), and yet, by presenting childhood as the connecting link, allows him a legitimate superiority to the children of mankind and to his own past.

In its contrasting pictures of childhood and age, the poem echoes a perennial theme of literature, formally embodied in the pastoral—the yearning of mankind for the state of Eden before the fall, the state of absolute security when the child is protected by his guardians. But perhaps because of Gray's natural temper, perhaps because of an unhappy childhood, it does not exhibit the sterile disgust with adulthood of Goldsmith's *Deserted Village* or such recent American classics as the fiction of Hemingway, where the chief theme is the purity of a Michigan boyhood destroyed by the dirty tricks played by age; Faulkner, who equates corruption with growing up; and Fitzgerald, whose most famous book is a monument to an adolescent dream.

Rather, Gray foreshadows the complex maturity of his admirer Blake, who sings the dewy joys of childhood in his "Songs of Innocence" but fashions a world in which man must progress beyond them. Unlike Blake, however, Gray sees no fruitful outcome for the adult. The ills of growth develop quite inevitably, and the poem does not give the impression of yearning for childhood—for one thing, the delusiveness of childhood joys is not merely stated, but stressed. Children are not idealized; they are happy (a state impossible for adults, Gray makes clear), but that is all. And as we have gathered from the "Ode to Adversity" and from his letters, Gray's ideal is not happiness but virtue; virtue, which for him above all demands sensitivity to the woes of others, comes only with adversity and adulthood.

A comment in a letter of some four years after the Eton College ode makes this point explicitly: "methinks I can readily pardon

Sickness & Age & Vexation for all the Depredations they make within & without, when I think they make us better Friends & better Men, wch I am persuaded is often the Case. I am very sure, I have seen the best-temper'd generous tender young Creatures in the World, that would have been very glad to be sorry for People they liked, when under any Pain, and could not; merely for Want of knowing rightly, what it was, themselves" (*C,* 1:248). The children's state, then, while joyful *for them,* is not to be envied by adults any more than the frisking of lambs before the slaughter is to be envied. Fate—and Elton's comparison to tragedy is peculiarly apt here—stands always ready to destroy.

The Eton College ode, more visibly than most other works by Gray, is absolutely symmetrical, the direction changing exactly in the middle (from line 50 to line 51). Through the first half, Gray describes the ignorant joys of his youth and of the children whom he now sees playing on the lawns and fields. Beginning with the first couplet of the second section, "Alas, regardless of their doom, The little victims play!" the catalog of woes develops. Just before this sudden clap, their joys have been most cheerfully caught: the quick recovery after tears, "The sunshine of the breast," the flourishing health, the vigor, the freshness of fancy, the eagerness for early rising to face the day. The section ends with morning's approach after easy sound sleep, with the coming of the enlivening sun. Then, suddenly, doom falls, at the very height of peace and freshness. Gray is evidently experimenting (successfully) with poetic effects again, this one of sudden shock anticipating the famous opening of "The Bard."

The second section also serves, as in all perfectly unified art, to give a new context and hence a richer meaning to the tone and feeling of the first. Elton noted, what indeed should have been obvious to anyone not bent on attacking Gray's ornate diction, that such phrases as "chase the rolling circle's speed" for "chase the hoop" are ironic. But is not all the poetic diction of the first part, as well as the setting and the apostrophe to the river and the hills, also at least partly ironic? The central quality of the poem, after all, is a kind of sympathetic irony: the children play in their delusive happiness in the first half, and we note and feel the pain of the reality in store for them in the second.

Moreover, the irony is accentuated in Richard Bentley's "Design" Frontispiece, which Walpole's note explains: "Boys at their sports,

Frontispiece for "Ode on a Distant Prospect of Eton College"

near the chapel of Eton, the god of the Thames sitting by: the passions, misfortunes, and diseases, coming down upon them. On either side, terms representing Jealousy and Madness. Above is a head of Folly: beneath, are play-things intermixed with thorns, a sword, a serpent and a scorpion." As Gray could of course see in this Design, the naked little boys are playing trifling, self-absorbed games, while the vicious woes of age come riding above through the clouds, armed and eager to attack them. Father Thames, stolidly bored, stretched out with his head leaning on an elbow, looks at a child who has just opened a cage with a bird in it, while two other boys swim near him. He does not even pretend to guard them. There is no question about the ironic intent of the drawing.

It seems to me that all of the triteness of language in the first half, and for that matter the triteness of situation, is in part an ironic allusion to the sort of poem that this *might* have been, to the host of poems celebrating the heedless joys of childhood. Here and there, in addition to the marked difference in diction between the first and second parts, the irony is hinted at. The opening stanza, for example, calls up all the grand elements—natural, physically and intellectually man-made, historic, even spiritual—that might guarantee the school's lasting protection of its wards' spirits: but stable and honorable as these are, none of them, not hills or holy founder or knowledge, even merits recollection when the second half exhibits the agony of maturity. For that matter, the whole formal experience of the college is irrelevant to the essential problems of being human. The fields in line 12 are "belov'd in vain": useless in the fight against fate. The gales blowing from the hills, shades, and fields offer only "a momentary bliss"—useless in the long run. The first section, then, combines a genuine appreciation of the vista and of man's attempts to evade mortality through charity and education with an ironic awareness of the brevity of their effectiveness; of their insignificance in the losing battle that man's hopes and illusions fight with fate. The diction, doing its share, steadily indicates the insufficiency of any poetic tradition that knows only one simple tone.

In the second section, the straightforwardly grim language is supported by a series of even grimmer personifications. In it Gray has gone far beyond the rather dull abstractions of the "Ode to Adversity" to a direct feeling for the "murth'rous band," a feeling that, if it does not justify, at least explains the period's admiration of the personification as the most condensed and sublime metaphor. In a line or two, sometimes in a phrase, he sketches the bitter qualities without wasting a syllable, and with the picture drawn before us: "Shame that sculks behind"; "Jealousy with rankling tooth, / That inly gnaws the secret heart"; "Ambition this shall tempt to rise, / Then whirl the wretch from high," etc. Within the context of Gray's aesthetic, these are clearly and vitally pictures—"sublime" horror pictures—not dead abstractions.

The concluding stanza, giving the reflections clearly derivable from the pictures in the preceding nine stanzas, ties the two parts together in a diction as smooth, clear, and ordinary (in the sense that Wordsworth wants the speech of ordinary men in his *Lyrical Ballads*) as is anywhere to be found in the language:

> To each his suff'rings: all are men,
> Condemn'd alike to groan,
> The tender for another's pain;
> Th'unfeeling for his own.
> Yet ah! why should they know their fate?
> Since sorrow never comes too late,
> And happiness too swiftly flies.
> Thought would destroy their paradise.
> No more; where ignorance is bliss,
> 'Tis folly to be wise.

The effect of the poem, on the picturesque level, is of fifty lines of sunshine occasionally threatened by clouds (or with the clouds latent) and of fifty lines of hellish storm. Gray at this point, the summer of his most acute unhappiness, does not yet balance the two pictures with as much complexity as in the "Elegy." His theme doess not call for the steady balance, except in the shades of tone to be derived from diction and structure; he can come to no more hopeful conclusion than the suffering in mutual charity of the "Ode to Adversity." It has been observed by some of Gray's most perceptive critics that his extraordinary sense of formal craftsmanship makes every stanza of a completed poem both perfectly discrete and organically relevant. Every one is complete within itself but at the same time contains the seeds of the next one and a development of what came before.[19] The stanza in the Eton College ode is again an intricate and experimental one, particularly useful for Gray's purposes. The central couplet often serves for the thesis of the stanza;

the quatrain on either side closes in what leads to it and what derives from it. The rhyme of the ending quatrain closes the stanza without either the emphatic pause of a couplet or the excessive separateness which a repetition of the alternating rhyme of the first quatrain might achieve.

To see the nature of the stanzaic units and their relationship to each other, consider the third stanza:

> Say, Father THAMES, for thou hast seen
> Full many a sprightly race
> Disporting on thy margent green
> The paths of pleasure trace,
> Who foremost now delight to cleave
> With pliant arm thy glassy wave?
> The captive linnet which enthrall?
> What idle progeny succeed
> To chase the rolling circle's speed,
> Or urge the flying ball?

Complete in itself as a question to Father Thames, it is also tied in the narrative to the earlier description of the river's intimacy with the scene; it forms the necessary connection between the river and the mood and picture which have caused the reflections and which dominate the first section. The stanza is connected as well to the next two, which extend its idealized actions symbolic of youth's heedlessnesss and the generalized reflections arising from them. Similarly, every other stanza is both separate and integrated within the poem. We might, if we wished, conclude that the reflections are not profound, that—as Johnson said—Gray thinks of no general point not available to anyone else; but we cannot condemn any aspect of the poem as artistically insufficient or irrelevant.

"Ode on the Death of a Favourite Cat, Drowned in a Tub of Gold Fishes"

The only poem that Gray completed between those of 1742 and the "Elegy" is his burlesque "Ode on the Death of a Favourite Cat" (1747). When Gray, now reconciled with Horace Walpole, heard of the drowning of his friend's cat, he wrote his most finished piece of versified playfulness. As was to be expected, this self-parody has aroused varying responses from readers, beginning with immense success among contemporary poetasters, whose tears, according to the *Critical Review* of 1768, "were for a long time employed upon linnets and larks that were shot, and parrots and bullfinches that were starved; upon dead lap-dogs, and drowned kittens."[20] Johnson was not amused:

> The poem on the Cat was doubtless by its author considered as a trifle, but it is not a happy trifle. In the first stanza "the azure flowers that blow" shew resolutely a rhyme is sometimes made when it cannot easily be found. Selima, the Cat, is called a nymph, with some violence both to language and sense; but there is good use made of it when it is done; for of the two lines,
>
> What female heart can gold despise?
> What cat's averse to fish?
>
> the first relates merely to the nymph, and the second only to the cat. The sixth stanza contains a melancholy truth, that "a favourite has no friend"; but the last ends in a pointed sentence of no relation to the purpose: if what glistered had been "gold," the cat would not have gone into the water; and, if she had, would not less have been drowned.[21]

Lord David Cecil, just as arbitrarily determined to be pleased by a poem that makes no intellectual demands on the reader, claims that it is "in its own brief way as enchanting a mixture of wit and prettiness as *The Rape of the Lock* itself." Roger Martin, who also likes the poem, though this side idolatry, points out that it is in a tradition of burlesques of funeral poems going back to the Greek anthology, a collection that was a favorite with Gray. More recently, Robert Pattison has seen it as a lesson in epistemology, a Lockean allegory of the mind studying its own operations; in the process, he shows that the surprising "Tyrian hue" of the goldfish (1.16) is plausible in terms of Newton's *Opticks*.[22]

Formally, we may note that Gray is once again using a stanza that he never repeats, practicing his careful weaving of unity through rhyme, mocking the grandeur of the language with short, quick rhythms. And Oliver Elton makes clear that this poem is, in addition, a conscious burlesque of the poet's own style: "It contains all his own tricks—the apostrophe, the personification, the periphrastic dialect, and the concluding moral tag, not to speak of the dolphin and the Nereid who rub elbows with Tom and Susan. The rounded form and resonant speech of the serious odes are perfectly imitated."[23] The turn of the poem comes in the middle, as we would expect, when Selima stretches her paw. As in the later important poems, Gray is combining narrative and lyric in his ode, in the manner of Dryden's "Alexander's Feast" (to which his opening stanza alludes); he is giving an action and not only a picture for the reflections to illuminate.

The underlying situations, not surprisingly, reflect Gray's fear of intense commitment and his concern for the solitariness of the adventurer. Imagining the catastrophe, he provided the vision not only of gold (beauty and expense) and fish (tasty nourishment) but also, as Johnson neglected to note, of angel forms, which a poet might have found even harder to resist than a nymph or a cat:

> Still had she gaz'd; but 'midst the tide
> Two angel forms were seen to glide,
> The Genii of the stream:
> Their scaly armour's Tyrian hue
> Thro' richest purple to the view
> Betray'd a golden gleam.

Is this not, again, from a different perspective and in a different tone, the figure choosing between the ordinary and the special? Richard Bentley's Frontispiece, fairly glossed by Walpole's Explanation, shows the other animals acting more normally (allowing for a rococo imagination) and prudently than the heroine: "The cat standing on the brim of the tub, and endeavouring to catch a gold fish. Two caryatides of a river god stopping his ears to her cries, and a Destiny cutting the nine threads of life, are on each side. Above, is a cat's head between two expiring lamps, and over that two mouse-traps, between a mandarin-cat sitting before a Chinese pagoda, and angling for gold fish into a china jar; and another cat drawing up a net. At the bottom are mice enjoying themselves on the prospect of the cat's death; a lyre and pallet." In Gray's poem, the cat leaps from the edge for the fancied, the visionary (for the poet, who is imagining her), and drowns—deservedly, for its motives are selfish. As the "Ode to Adversity" and the Eton College ode had already shown, and as the "Elegy" and the Pindaric Odes were to show with greater sensitivity and power, the self Gray imagined could at its best find more humane direction.

Frontispiece for "Ode on the Death of a Favourite Cat, Drowned in a Tub of Gold Fishes"

Chapter Four
"Elegy Written in a Country Church-Yard"

Gray's "Elegy" was universally admired in his lifetime and has remained continuously the most popular of mid-eighteenth-century English poems; it is, as Gosse has called it, the standard English poem. The reasons for this extraordinary unanimity of praise are as varied as the ways in which poetry can appeal. The "Elegy" is a beautiful technical accomplishment, as can be seen even in such details as the variation of the vowel sounds or the poet's rare discretion in the choice of adjectives and adverbs. Its phrasing is both elegant and memorable, as is evident from the incorporation of much of it into the living language. It is sympathetically concerned with social issues, primarily with the differences in the fate of rich and poor, and this in image patterns that have been found rewarding by the highly technical critics of our century. Its tone is perfectly maintained, combining the dignity and pathos most suitable for its function, a reflection on death and life. It fulfills the eighteenth-century ideal—still a valid one for poetry—of expressing a general state important for all men, a condition of existence that we must all anticipate. That is to say, it establishes universal truths; and it recognizably connects the personal feeling of the poet to this universal feeling of all mankind.

The specific time at which Gray wrote the "Elegy" is not certain. Mason, in his combined *Memoirs* and edition of Gray, gives the circumstances of the writing as he conjectures them: "I am inclined to believe that the Elegy in a Country Church-yard was begun, if not concluded, at this time also [at the death of West]: Though I am aware that, as it stands at present, the conclusion is of a later date."[1] Mason's closeness to the poet makes his guess—and it is no more—worth noting. However, Mason did not know Gray in 1742 and apparently never asked him when he wrote his masterpiece. Walpole, who was intimately involved in its publication, says in his brief "Memoir of Gray" that it was finished in 1750 (*C,* 3:1287);

a letter from Gray to Walpole of 12 June 1750 says he is sending a poem he has just finished. There is, therefore, no reason to assume that the poem was written earlier than the 1746–50 period, when Gray's letters refer to it, though some scholars have continued to see it as an immediate response to West's death.[2]

Mason's note on the "Elegy" in his edition of Gray gives us further useful information:

> The most popular of all our Author's publications; it ran through eleven editions in a very short space of time; was finely translated into Latin by Messrs. Ansty and Roberts; and in the same year another, though I think inferior, version of it was published by Mr. Lloyd. . . . He [Gray] originally gave it only the simple title of "Stanzas written in a Country Church-yard." I persuaded him first to call it an ELEGY, because the subject authorized him so to do; and the alternate measure, in which it was written, seemed peculiarly fit for that species of composition. I imagined too that so capital a Poem, written in this meausre, would as it were appropriate it in future to writings of this sort; and the number of imitations which have since been made of it (even to satiety) seem to prove that my notion was well founded. In the first manuscript copy of this exquisite Poem, I find the conclusion different from that which he afterwards composed; and tho' his after-thought was unquestionably the best, yet there is a pathetic melancholy in the four rejected stanzas, which highly claims preservation.[3]

As Mason implies, Gray's contemporaries sang a unified chorus of praise, in which even Johnson joined: "The *Church-yard* abounds with images which find a mirror in every mind, and with sentiments to which every bosom returns an echo. . . . Had Gray written often thus it had been vain to blame, and useless to praise him."[4]

Poetic Tradition

One reason for this response was the contemporary awareness of the poetic tradition behind the "Elegy," which Amy Louise Reed has so admirably described in *The Background of Gray's Elegy*. In the seventeenth century, she shows, melancholy was a favorite poetic theme, particularly in a setting of the countryside; both theme and setting echo similar poems of the classical period. In the early eighteenth century, "the melancholy of the preceding age persists and the old subjects are treated with even more diffuseness. There is the same fascination with the thought of death, suicide, physical decay, and the Great Assize, the same complaint of the vanity of life, the same professed admiration for solitary retirement. Point of view and phrasing are still largely subject to the same literary influences, Lucretius, Virgil, Horace, Seneca, Martial, *Ecclesiastes, Job,* the *Psalms,* reinforced by the influence of Milton."[5] The last reference is of course primarily to Milton's "Il Penseroso."

As Reed points out, William Shenstone, a minor contemporary of Gray, most clearly discussed the tradition of the English elegy up to his own time in "A Prefatory Essay on Elegy." Elegy, he wrote, "includes a tender and querulous idea . . . it looks upon this as its peculiar characteristic, and so long as this is thoroughly sustained, admits of a variety of subjects; which by its manner of treating them, it renders its own. It throws its melancholy stole over pretty different objects; which, like the dresses at a funeral procession, gives them all a kind of solemn and uniform appearance." The form is unsuitable for ribald love poetry, he says, but it will do for almost "any kind of subjects, treated in such a manner as to diffuse a pleasing melancholy. . . ." Of these subjects, "it is in particular the task and merit of elegy to shew the innocence and simplicity of rural life to advantage. . . ." Elegy, he summarizes, is "A kind of poetry that magnifies the sweets of liberty and independence, that endears the honest delights of love and friendship, that celebrates the glory of a good name after death, that ridicules the futile arrogance of birth, that recommends the innocent amusement of letters, and insensibly prepares the mind for that humanity it inculcates. . . ."[6] One might think that Shenstone was writing a prescription for duplicating Gray's poem.[7]

Another element substantially contributing to context, to amplify Reed's comments, was the development in the mid-eighteenth century of a gloomy group of English poets now usually referred to as the Graveyard School. Deriving partly from melancholy reflections on man's fate that were always available and exploited by poets and preachers, partly from the propaganda of revivalist sects of the seventeenth and eighteenth centuries, and partly from the defensive response of religion to the rational Deism and atheism prevalent among the educated upper classes early in the century, the poetry of this school consisted largely of horrifying poetic sermons. Of these, the most successful was Edward Young's *Night Thoughts,* a long work in which a gay rake called Lorenzo is graphically warned, primarily by the sight of the moldering bones of the dead, of the coming reckoning. Though a modern critic has pointed out that the poem's "great value lay in its view of death as a challenge to intensified life,"[8] its contemporary reader, like the modern one, was probably most impressed by the horrors rather than by the challenge of death. Both would have been made vivid by the major event in England in 1745 (when the last installment of *Night Thoughts* appeared) and 1746, the Jacobite rebellion led by Charles Edward ("Bonnie Prince Charlie"), the son of the Stuart claimant of the British throne. (Gray had seen both father and son a few years earlier at receptions in Italy.) It was crushed with great brutality at Culloden in spring 1746, and followed by public trials of the Scottish lords, some of which Gray attended while visiting London: object lessons in where the paths of glory led.

To return to poetic tradition, the iambic pentameter quatrain with alternating rhyme (because of which Mason persuaded Gray to incorporate "elegy" in the title) was peculiarly associated with the elegiac form in the eighteenth century through the efforts of the minor poet James Hammond. Hammond borrowed most of his substance and tone from the Roman elegiac poet Tibullus,[9] who had been a favorite with West during the last few years of his life. The elegiac form thus had widespread contemporary precedent, personal allusiveness, and another element most important to Gray as technician: classical authority in the writings of the Romans. As Oliver Elton has pointed out, the "Elegy" is peculiarly notable for echoing "the classical elegiac, with its *inscriptional* character. Nearly all the stanzas of the *Elegy* are self-contained in grammar and meaning; most of them could go well upon a tablet in a church wall. . . ."[10] And as Lonsdale notes (*P,* 115), Gray's poem contains many allusions to one of Virgil's *Georgics* and Horace's second *Epode,* two works celebrating retirement widely known and admired in the period. To summarize, the "Elegy" comes as the culmination of a variety of traditions, both contemporary and ancient: another way of saying that it expresses certain experiences and responses that seem permanent aspects of human life. At the same time, it symbolically condenses Gray's own experiences and his reflections on them: from Eton on, for example, he had known and weighed himself against the rich and powerful; he was turning thirty, having achieved nothing important (he thought his law degree derisory); and he was contemplating a changeless, obscure life in Cambridge.

Interpretations

Since 1751, the "Elegy" has maintained its eminence with critics as well as with general readers, though it now seems not so simple a poem as its early admirers thought. Earlier this century the notable critic William Empson attacked its social views as quietistic, and several critics have doubted its unity. To the questions of unity and social justice have at times been added other important questions about the relevance of the first manuscript, the nature of the language, the identity of the narrator, the subject of the "Epitaph," and the "thee" of line 93. The more closely the poem is scrutinized, the more uncertainty there is about what actually happens in it.

In *Some Versions of Pastoral* Empson found in the "Elegy"—particularly in the "Full many a gem" stanza—social snobbery and heartless unconcern for the poor, surely a strange charge against a poem of which an immediate abridger, the *British Magazine* of February 1751, observed, "The just regard shewn by the author to humble stations and the unheeded usefulness of rustic industry, may tend to repress that pride which the petty superiority of our present state too frequently excites."[11] As might be expected of Empson, his argument is subtle:

> By comparing the social arrangement to Nature he makes it seem inevitable, which it was not, and gives it a dignity which was undeserved. Furthermore, a gem does not mind being in a cave and a flower prefers not to be picked; we feel that the man is like the flower, as short-lived, natural, and valuable, and this tricks us into feeling that he is better off without opportunities. The sexual suggestion of *blush* brings in the Christian idea that virginity is good in itself, and so that any renunciation is good; this may trick us into feeling it is lucky for the poor man that society keeps him unspotted from the world. The tone of melancholy claims that the poet understands the considerations opposed to aristocracy, though he judges against them; the truism of the reflections in the churchyard, the universality and impersonality this gives to the style, claim as if by comparison that we ought to accept the injustice of society as we do the inevitability of death.[12]

Cleanth Brooks's analysis, summarized below, very competently disposes of Empson's attack; more can, however, be said on the subject of the specific image that Empson uses as the basis of his interpretation. How he learns the motives of gems and flowers I do not know. But the evidence strongly suggests that for Gray (as for his master Plato) self-realization is the deepest right of man. His political poem "The Alliance of Education and Government" stresses the need for society to be organized so that talents will not be wasted, and he there uses the very images of gem and flower to make his point. The images recur in "Ode for Music," again for the same purpose. While it is possible that Gray meant these examples for one purpose in the "Elegy" and another in other poems, such difference is nowhere implied. Furthermore, all of Gray's work expresses a yearning for individual fulfillment on his own part and a resentment against any forces which repress such fulfillment. Whatever the "Elegy's" long-run message dealing with humanity at large may be—and the poem is meaningless if it does not transcend social divisions and apply to all mankind—the immediate sympathy is for the poor, and the immediate social issue of justice is settled in their favor.

The structural effect of the "Epitaph" and the identity of the narrator have been knottier problems than the determination of Gray's social sympathies. Of the three manuscripts in Gray's hand which remain, the earliest—the "Eton" one —includes four stanzas which came after the present line 72 and which, according to Mason, were to have ended the poem. These stanzas strongly suggest identification of the narrator with Gray. Since they introduce no major complications or developments, they have been considered by some critics as structurally superior to the 56 lines with which Gray replaced them.[13] It is dangerous to differ with so sober a critic as Lonsdale, who says that the existence of "two distinct versions" of the "Elegy" is "the crucial fact about the poem" (*P,* 114), but two considerations force me to do so: (1) The most certain thing about rejected passages and abandoned fragments is that they are rejected, and Gray treated the earlier version as a fragment. Rejected materials, even so fine as the Eton manuscript of the "Elegy," provide private pleasures to the scholar and, used with caution, may help to point out elements in what has enriched life—the public, completed work. (2) The version provided by Walpole and printed by Dodsley in 1751 and widely reprinted in magazines, corrected in relatively minor ways by Gray for the *Six Poems* of 1753 and the *Poems* of 1768, is the poem the world has so long known and loved; therefore, necessarily the achieved work of art; therefore, irrespective of academic eccentricities, the version to be discussed.

In 1947, Cleanth Brooks included in his *Well Wrought Urn* one of the best discussions that we have. Brooks is concerned with the relation of parts in the poem as they elucidate its thought and make of it a whole. He begins by examining the scene: "What the attention is focused on, even in the first stanzas, is not the graveyard itself, but what can be seen by a man standing in the graveyard"—note here the echo of the technique of the Eton College ode. The churchyard is mainly described "by contrast with its opposite: the great abbey church," with more details given of the interior of the church—though it is not physically within view of the observer, he is presumably imagining it—than of the yard. Developing this point, Brooks says that "the personifications are actually the allegoric figures, beloved by the eighteenth century, which clutter a great abbey church such as that at Bath or at Westminster."[14] These personifications are intended "to seem empty, flat, and lifeless" in contrast to the burial places of the poor, and many of them, such as Honour, are used ironically.

The line "Their sober wishes never learn'd to stray," according to Brooks, is a "careful inversion of the usual terms. One expects straying to be 'natural,' not something to be learned. One 'learns' to *refrain* from straying. Knowledge has therefore conferred a favor, whatever her intentions, in refusing to unroll 'to their eyes her ample page.' For what Knowledge has to give is associated with madness, not sobriety." The abbey and the churchyard are "drawn together" in stanza 20, where the poet speaks of various memorials, rhymes, etc., of the poor; this is an objective view, since it makes both the poor attempts and the ornate memorials "the expression of a basic human impulse." The comment on death emphasizes the union of common humanity: "The impulse to hold on to life—to strive against the encompassing oblivion—is to be found under the 'yew-tree's shade' as well as beneath the 'fretted vault.' If the one has been treated with more pathos, the other with more irony, still neither can be effectual, and both in their anguish of attempt are finally deeply human."[15]

In stanza 24, Brooks continues, the poet-observer (the "me" of the first stanza) is considering himself: "Dramatically, what has happened is that the meditation has gone on so fervently that in talking to himself, the speaker has lost his identity as an ego. The commentary which has been going on, though it has begun as that of the solitary observer, has become more general, more external."

The last part of the poem is its resolution: "first, we have had the case of those who could not choose, the 'rude Forefathers of the hamlet'; next, the Proud, who chose, but chose in vanity; lastly, there is the present case, the man who is able to choose, and chooses the 'neglected spot' after all." [16] And here, supporting Brooks's examination, Bentley's *Designs* Frontispiece shows rich and poor emphatically contrasted (subject to the reminder of mortality in the scene at the center and the clock tower behind it), as we can further note from Walpole's explanation: "A Gothic gateway in ruins with the emblems of nobility on one side; on the other, the implements and employments of the Poor. Thro' the arch appears a church-yard and village-church built out of the remains of an abbey. A countryman showing an epitaph to a passenger." In the "Epitaph" ending the poem, Brooks says, the first line "implies the choice" referred to—he will be buried in the yard, not inside the church—and "Melancholy becomes thus, in association with Science, a kind of wisdom which allows him to see through the vanities which delude the Proud."[17] In this way, the epitaph is integral to the overall structure of the poem.

Another major contribution to full understanding of the "Elegy" was an article by Frank H. Ellis, "Gray's *Elegy:* The Biographical Problem in Literary Criticism," which appeared in 1951. Ellis argues that in the original form, "The *Stanza's wrote in a country churchyard* were . . . an 'artless Tale' about Thomas Gray, not about 'th' unhonour'd Dead,' just as *Lycidas* is essentially a 'Doric lay' about John Milton, not about the 'Unwept' Edward King. Both poems are concerned with the same themes: the alienation of the Poet from his audience, or the conflict between the aesthetic values of poetry and the materialistic values of 'the World,' which were already conventional themes in the poetry of Theocritus." In the revision of the poem, however, Gray "depersonalized" it; and he therefore had to produce "a conclusion which shifted the bearing of the poem from the Poet to the rustics."[18] The poem, I may add parenthetically, invites all sorts of speculation about the subject of its "Epitaph," the most startling suggestion being that of Odell Shepard, who in 1923 proposed Richard West. Although this thesis cannot be effectively maintained, it was immensely useful in spurring closer analysis of the events and characters of the "Elegy."[19]

Like the earlier draft, Ellis argues, the revised "Elegy" is modeled on *Lycidas:* "In the original *Stanza's,* the narrator, with whom Gray identified himself, occupied the central position of the 'uncouth Swain' who mourns for Lycidas. But in the completed *Elegy,* the Spokesman is relegated to the position of the anonymous elegist whom the 'uncouth Swain' in *Lycidas* momentarily invokes, and the central position is occupied by the village Stonecutter who mourns 'th' unhonour'd Dead.' Gray has shifted the bearing of the poem from the conflict of the Poet with an alien world to the triumphant persistence, or continuity, of poetry, despite this hostile world. And this is what may be implied in the concluding lines of *Lycidas:* 'To morrow to fresh Woods and Pastures new.' "[20]

The poem is a reflective one, says Ellis, and the theme of the reflection is the contrast of the "ruling classes" with the "rural proletariat." The attitudes toward them are "developed through the Spokesman, who . . . identifies himself with neither class,"[21] his reactions being quite complex. In the poetical structure, "The imagined death of the peasant-poet supplies the dramatic example which illustrates and makes cogent the large generalities of the previous argument. The case-history of the village Stonecutter should make the reader *feel* what previously the poem simply *stated,* namely, what it is to be a poet *manqué,* a 'mute inglorious Milton' possessed of a 'noble Rage,' which is drowned in poverty, ignorance, lack of sympathy and scope."[22] Besides discussing diction with more or less illumination, criticism in the past thirty years has largely responded to or elaborated on the views of Brooks and Ellis, which have brilliantly justified the unity of tone and structure of the poem.[23]

Perhaps to all of this analysis may be added a few additional scattered observations on the structure of the "Elegy." In it Gray seems to have been at great pains to bring the turn to the reader's attention: not only does he change overt subjects at this point, but he makes the middle one of the very few places in which the grammatical and logical sense of one stanza runs over into another. Of the finished poem's 128 lines, here are lines 61–68:

Th' applause of list'ning senates to command,
The threats of pain and ruin to despise,
To scatter plenty o'er a smiling land,
And read their hist'ry in a nation's eyes,

Their lot forbad: nor circumscrib'd alone
Their growing virtues, but their crimes confin'd;

> Forbad to wade through slaughter to a throne,
> And shut the gates of mercy on mankind. . . .

Though the next stanza is grammatically connected to this one, and though later, at another significant turn (ll. 93–100), a sentence is divided between two stanzas, nowhere else in the poem does Gray use this emphatically periodic enjambment of two stanzas. And, with an artist as conscious of effects as Gray, there is no room to doubt the deliberateness of his intention: he wanted to force on the reader, and perhaps on himself, the moral advantages of obscurity. The epitaph is a repetition, on an individual scale, of the increased possibilities for virtue in solitude.

The other significant place where stanzas are grammatically connected—lines 93–100, three quarters of the way through—ties the life of the Stonecutter (Gray's other self by any reckoning) to the customs of society:

> For thee, who mindful of th' unhonour'd Dead
> Dost in these lines their artless tale relate;
> If chance, by lonely contemplation led,
> Some kindred Spirit shall inquire thy fate,
>
> Haply some hoary-headed Swain may say,
> 'Oft have we seen him at the peep of dawn
> 'Brushing with hasty steps the dews away
> 'To meet the sun upon the upland lawn.'

Whether Gray's syntax directs us to the Stonecutter seems irrelevant; clearly, to judge by the poems discussed earlier, Gray himself was being justified.

The structure is actually not at all far from that of the "Ode on the Spring," as Mason implied in suggesting that Gray thought of one as a poem on noon, the other on evening. At first we observe quiet, restful nature around the spokesman for the poet. Here are the same farmer, cows, birds, and insects, except that, in keeping with the greater solemnity and stillness, we are shown only one insect and one bird. The spokesman then surveys mankind, this time in retrospect or imagination rather than with the physical eye. A huge difference, of course, is the relative position of Gray vis-à-vis humanity at the conclusion. Here, like Meursault in Albert Camus's *The Stranger,* Gray finds himself united with humanity through the fact of death, in an ending that breathes rest and completion rather than the self-pity of the earlier poem. Again, Bentley's Frontispiece leads us to this vision, for the passerby talking to the rustic over the gravestone himself casts a shadow "across the grave he enquires about," as Irene Tayler has noted; and Margaret Anne Doody goes further to say that "the poet's shadow, cast along the grave whose monument he observes, indicates and literally foreshadows his own destiny. . . ."[24]

A number of subordinate techniques have contributed to the mood of acceptance of the "Elegy." Although the poem moves from life to death, it also moves from dusk to morning, with all of it from line 97 taking place in an imagined morning context. Furthermore, Gray is careful to suggest life around the graves and in the past of their occupants. The very presence of the farmer, cows, beetle, and owl in the opening stanzas implies the steady, though subdued, vitality provided by nature's routine. The description of what will *not* awaken or respond to the dead is further full of fresh and natural noises and movements, of a recurring vitality:

> The breezy call of incense-breathing Morn,
> The swallow twitt'ring from the straw-built shed,
> The cock's shrill clarion, or the echoing horn,
> No more shall rouse them from their lowly bed.
>
> For them no more the blazing hearth shall burn,
> Or busy housewife ply her evening care:
> No children run to lisp their sire's return,
> Or climb his knees the envied kiss to share.

There is action, life in every phrase—an action and a life and a color that endure through the generations. Even in the description of the graveyard and the barrows raised by the bodies, Gray uses his celebrated skill with sounds to suggest movement and energy: when he says that there "heaves the turf in many a mould'ring heap," the very moldering is contradicted by the powerful movement stressed by the alliteration and assonance. Even in the traditional image of death that Bentley offers in his Tailpiece, the torch expiring in the vault, the fire's vigor reaches out in smoke to the sky.

The justification of the lives of the dead, beginning with the stanzas so marked by the main turn, easily leads to the description of the justifier, the "artless" retailer of their tale. This storyteller

Tailpiece for "Elegy Written in a Country Church-Yard"

in stone is certainly Gray, though at one remove—the sameness of their function really admits of no more than quibbling about the identity of the peasant poet. The psychological distance gained by the creation of the Stonecutter seems intended to allow Gray without sentimentality to shed a tear for his own existence. For Gray, as I have suggested, exactly the same justification had been developing: he saw himself as poor, obscure, more than usually acceptable for "Science" (learning), melancholy, and ambitions of being good—of feeling for the sorrows of others. Moreover, while the Stonecutter has failed to project himself beyond the small village circle, that group is an epitome of mankind, and he is amply distinguished within it. We are given the effect, much to be desired in a poem tying mankind together through the continuity of the generations under a just God, of a series of mirrors: Gray looks to his own fate, and finds the Stonecutter; behind the Stonecutter are the poor subjects of his unlettered muse; and behind the "short and simple annals of the poor" lies the contrasting opposite, which in the long run is no more than an alternate equivalent, "all that beauty, all that wealth e'er gave"—in short, mankind, very possibly reflected back in the routine of the plowman. As Lawrence Lipking observes, "When the 'hoary-headed swain' invites the 'kindred spirit' to 'Approach and read' . . . he beckons the reader also into the picture. We all approach and read . . . the epitaph: the line between what is inside and outside the poem fades away. Gray sees himself as if he were another and we see Gray as if he were ourselves. The effect is totally absorbing. In that moment the poet achieves the point of view he has been seeking: a vision of the churchyard so sympathetic that all of us can share it and see ourselves there."[25]

Several points still need to be made about the "Elegy," one of those rich poems that yield more as one examines them more. Its ironic effects are particularly worth investigating, as they affect its structure and diction. In his article, Ellis correctly commented that the Stonecutter and his "Epitaph" are idealized examples of the preceding generalizations. But if, as he believes, the Stonecutter is an idealized representation of the man driven melancholy mad by contemplating the inevitable end of all men, then the movement of the poem is an ironical refutation of this surface pessimism: in the poem the Stonecutter's fame lives on—if only for a little while—and at the end he is surrounded by sunshine.

Also, Brooks' observation that Gray's diction is often ironic is worth elaborating. In the "Elegy," as might be expected, Gray perfects the technique that he had previously used for structural effect mainly in the "Ode on the Spring" and in the Eton College ode. In the "Elegy" his deliberately ornate imagery begins with stanza 5, "The breezy call," where Gray is allusively emphasizing the fact that these poetic evocations will *not* call up the peasants who are dead. The descriptions of the great involve immense irony—implicit in their fates—and are expressed in a language reeking of the poetry of the past that is self-consciously and deliberately swollen: "The boast of heraldry, the pomp of pow'r," etc. The eleventh stanza, which as Brooks says evokes the impressions of great Gothic abbeys, heavily underscores the irony:

Can storied urn or animated bust
Back to its mansion call the fleeting breath?
Can Honour's voice provoke the silent dust,
Or Flatt'ry sooth the dull cold ear of Death?

The succeeding stanzas, outlining what great things the poor might have done if given the chance, stress both the essential equivalence and the essential unimportance of the achievements missed—and in glowing language. The irony again becomes manifest in the two stanzas beginning with "Some village Hampden." In general, Gray is using his practiced, delicate device of heightening, almost burlesquing the language, by filling it with epic implications to suggest by contrast the triviality of all but virtue. Here is a subtle and hence easily misunderstood use of a device more evident in Pope's "Rape of the Lock," where epic diction for petty events emphasizes the *lack* of heroic qualities in the society described. It is all the more remarkable that in the "Elegy," Gray is able to command language so as to achieve effects similar to those of the "Ode on the Spring" and to the Eton College ode while at the same time avoiding triteness. From the point of view of diction the poem is both a dignified tribute to the recurring cycles of human life, inevitably lost in obscurity while it vainly seeks earthly immortality, and an ironic commentary on that very seeking—at least in its socially admired forms.

More generally, the "Elegy" is a poem reflecting on the eternal truths connected with death; but it is far richer than that, or it would not have survived any more than have other melancholy effusions of its day. It is a reflection on loneliness, but with that state resolved into the much more hopeful awareness of the community of mankind. It suggests strongly an affirmation of life and an assurance of the continuity of life, of man's connection both with nature and with other men. Most poignantly, it expresses the wish of the poet to see himself as one with man's destiny, which he accepts while he is aware that it cannot be defined on earth. His fundamental, recurrent question about the purpose of his life (first poetically explored in the "Ode on the Spring") has found its universally resonant expression.

Chapter Five
The Pindaric Odes

No other poems completed by Gray so closely reflect his academic pursuits as the "Wonderful Wonder of Wonders, the two Sister Odes," as Johnson called them, which are at the same time his most original and adventurous performances. W. Powell Jones, elucidating Gray's immense scholarly studies, shows that Gray was kept busy during the late 1740s and early 1750s compiling an encyclopedic chronology of all the events of classical Greece for a period of several hundred years. In 1753 and afterwards, Gray set himself the study of poetics, preparing to work on a history of English poetry. As Jones says, a scholar like Gray inevitably reached back into Provençal and Italian literatures for the roots of English poetry, and inevitably was forced back to the Greeks and particularly to Pindar, the greatest of their lyric poets. From this study, says Jones, "The result is 'An Ode in the Greek Manner,' since known as *The Progress of Poesy*. In 1747 Gray had made a thorough analysis of Pindar's metres, and so he was able to show, as nearly as one could in English verse, what a genuine Pindaric ode should be."[1]

There was precedent for careful scholarship behind the English Pindaric, though the form had originally been introduced into popularity without regard for this heritage. In his *Pindaric Odes* (1656), Abraham Cowley, who had aimed at his model's wild loftiness without considering the strictness of his form, had produced the "irregular Pindarics," made up of long stanzas in which the lines arbitrarily differed in length and meter. Others, seeking similar effects, had similarly disregarded recurrent patterns, sometimes brilliantly (as in Dryden's "Alexander's Feast" and Killigrew Ode), but more often (as in Swift's early poems) with distressing results. In 1706, William Congreve, the great comic playwright, seems to have been the first Englishman to rediscover and proclaim the principles of Pindar's composition. He complains that there have been no true Pindarics so far and that "The character of these late Pindarics is, a bundle of rambling incoherent thoughts, expressed in a like parcel of irregular stanzas, which also consist of such another complication of disproportioned, uncertain, and perplexed verses and rhymes."[2]

Congreve insists that Pindar's poems were regular in form: his odes "were sung by a chorus, and adapted to the lyre, and sometimes to the lyre and pipe: they consisted oftenest of three stanzas; the first was called the strophe, from the version or circular motion of the singers in that stanza from the right hand to the left. The second stanza was called the antistrophe, from the contraversion of the chorus; the singers, in performing that, turning from the left hand to the right, contrary always to their motion in the strophe. The third stanza was called the epode . . . which they sung in the middle, neither turning to one hand nor the other."[3] Congreve also insists that following Pindar's practice, the strophes and antistrophes must have the same metrical pattern in any one poem, though the epodes may follow a different pattern. The regular Pindaric became fairly common after Congreve's essay and its accompanying sample, but William Collins and Gray were the first to write enduring poetry in this form.

The composition of these odes seems to have caused Gray unusual difficulty. Work on the first one went slowly, hindered partly by Gray's tendency to lose his inspiration on longer pieces, partly by Mason's contagious fear that the public would not find the poem clear. Gray was also bothered by the technical problems connected with achieving unity within a complex form. He apologized to Bedingfield for not sending him a copy of the poem: "to abate your curiosity I assure you it is very incorrect, & being wrote by fits & starts at very distant intervals is so unequal that it will hardly admit of particular corrections. . . . I have written part of another, wch intends to be much better, but my Inspiration is very apt to fail me before I come to a conclusion" (*C,* 2:462). After showing around the poems, he complained that some people "like the first Ode (that has no Tout-Ensemble) the best of the two" (*C,* 2:503–4). Posterity has on the whole justified Gray's preference for the second.

When the *Odes* were published, Gray kept hearing of readers who were puzzled (for example, *C,* 2:519). As W. Powell Jones has shown, it was equally fashionable to buy the *Odes* and complain about their unintelligibility.[4] Sensitive to the public despite scorning its judgment, Gray provided notes for a later edition: "as to the notes, I do it out of spite, because the Publick did not understand the two odes (wch I have call'd Pindaric) tho' the first was not very dark, & the second alluded to a few common facts to be found in any six-penny History of England by way of question & answer for the use of children" (*C,* 3:1002).

But there were important champions too. David Garrick, the great and popular actor-director, wrote a poem "To Mr. Gray, upon his Odes" for the *London Chronicle* of 29 September–1 October 1757 stressing their search for the sublime when popular taste was being stultified by "the gentle Muse / That little dares, and little means." The *Critical Review*'s man, though confused over Aeolian lyre and Aeolian harp, was "in raptures" (*C,* 2:526). A spirited public defense of the poem against "the dunces" is particularly interesting because it appeared in the *Literary Magazine* (September–October and October–November 1757), with which Johnson had been closely associated a few months before. After justifying several phrases that had been objected to—among them "many-twinkling feet" and "weave the warp and weave the woof," which Johnson still disliked a quarter century later—the reviewer praises the first ode for "Sublimity of conception, a nobleness in his diction, daring figures, quick transition, harmony of numbers, and an enthusiasm that hurries the reader along with him."[5] Still, like Gray himself, he prefers the *Bard,* and if he were not afraid of being pompous, "We should say that it contains all the species of eloquence which *Longinus* makes the constituents of the sublime, namely; 1st, an elevation of sentiment, 2d, a pathetic vehemence, 3d, a bold combination of figures, 4th, a splendid diction, and 5th, a beautiful harmony of parts in the whole composition."[6]

One member of the reading public whose complaint deserved attention was Oliver Goldsmith, then an irreverent young man trying to make his way into the literary world. In his review of the *Odes* for the *Monthly Review* of September, 1757, he complains that, while Gray is clearly an extraordinary poet, he ought to write for mankind at large rather than for the chosen few, the literati. He also gives Gray gratuitous advice (which the poet ironically cited in a letter): "such a genius as Mr. Gray might give greater pleasure, and acquire a larger portion of fame, if, instead of being an imitator, he did justice to his talents, and ventured to be more an original."[7] Goldsmith continues with comments which are both perceptive and useful to introduce a discussion of the poems: "The first of these Poems celebrates the Lyric Muse. It seems the most laboured performance of the two; but yet we think its merit is not equal to that of the second. It seems to want that regularity of plan upon which the second is founded; and though it abounds with images that strike, yet, unlike the second, it contains none that are affecting."[8] These are essentially the reasons for which Gray himself preferred the second ode.

"The Progress of Poesy"

Since "The Progress of Poesy" retains some obscurities despite the passage of years, it may be helpful to explicate it. The poem is divided into three groups (triads or ternaries); and each group has three stanzas, the strophe, antistrophe, and epode. The opening image is intended as a recognizable echo of Pindar, as Gray's note makes very clear: "Pindar styles his own poetry with its musical accompanyments. . . . Æolian song, Æolian strings, the breath of the Æolian flute . . . The subject and simile, as usual with Pindar, are united. The various sources of poetry, which gives life and lustre to all it touches, are here described; its quiet majestic progress enriching every subject (otherwise dry and barren) with a pomp of diction and luxuriant harmony of numbers; and its more rapid and irresistible course, when swoln and hurried away by the conflict of tumultuous passions" (*CP,* 205). Jean Hagstrum, in his perceptive study of the relations in the period between painting and poetry, best sums up the aim of this introductory stanza: "Gray was not interested in stating meaning directly or in giving clear, logical referents for his images. He wanted, first in a Claudian and then in a Salvatorian picture, to portray two antithetical conditions of music. . . ."[9] The poem afterwards, Hagstrum points out, becomes a series of picture panels.

Of the opening of the second stanza, Gray notes: "Power of harmony to calm the turbulent sallies of the soul. The thoughts are borrowed from the first Pythian of Pindar." Both Mars and Jove, representing forms of anger, are shown as calmed by music. Johnson's complaint here, as in all of his discussion of Gray's Pindaric Odes, is wildly unfair though quite funny: "The second stanza, exhibiting Mars's car and Jove's eagle, is unworthy of further notice. Criticism disdains to chase a school-boy to his common-places."[10] But Gray is not showing off his Greek. Rather, he is specifically alluding to Pindar's first Pythian, in which both images appear, as the pattern from which he is working. The reader is supposed to recollect or reread that poem and to appreciate Gray's evocation of its attitudes as support and decoration for his own.

Gray informs the reader, in his note to the opening of the first epode (third stanza of the first triad), that the subject is "Power of harmony to produce all the graces of motion in the body." It describes first a dance of Venus's ("Cytherea's") retinue on the mountain sacred to her (Idalia). In contrast to their "frisking," the goddess, a symbol of both love and harmony, is introduced in slow music and walks with a stately, easy grace. Color, as is obvious, everywhere supports the music, which is a reflection of the poetic statement. This stanza has been seen as one of Gray's most dazzling achievements. John Mitford, the best of Gray's early editors, says of it, for example: "The third stanza in the 'Progress of Poetry [*sic*],' descriptive of quick and joyous, and then slow and dignified motion, and the change of numbers and of sentiment in the last stanza, may be mentioned as fit instances to corroborate this assertion [that Gray's versification has a "peculiar harmony and variety"]: indeed, I think, with respect to the exquisite harmony of its movements, this poem is formed upon more delicate principles, and with more curious attention, than 'The Bard.' "[11] Mrs. David Garrick, herself a professional dancer, said of line 35 ("Glance their many-twinkling feet"), "Mr. Gray is the only poet who ever understood dancing" (*C,* 2:513, n. 5).

The second ternary opens with a concentrated echo of the poems of 1742 (notably the Eton College ode), for it lists the ills in store for man. But here Gray says that the complaint is a "fond" one—a foolish one, a deluded one—and he wishes to "justify the laws of Jove." Unlike Milton and Pope, to whose key lines in *Paradise Lost* and *An Essay on Man* this phrase alludes, Gray will do it neither by theology nor by philosophy, but by showing the inspirational effects of poetry. God means for these ills to dominate man only until man perceives Hyperion—the Sun, who here is equated with poetry—at which point the ills vanish. Gray's note says, "To compensate the real and imaginary ills of life, the Muse was given to Mankind by the same Providence that sends the Day by its chearful presence to dispel the gloom and terrors of the Night."

For the second stanza of this ternary, Gray notes: "Extensive influence of poetic Genius over the remotest and most uncivilized nations: its connection with liberty, and the virtues that naturally attend on it. (See the Erse, Norwegian, and Welch Fragments, the

Lapland and American songs.)" Even where, in perpetually ice-covered regions, the sun never comes, poetic harmony has brought light to cheer the native. In Chile, where sunlight cannot penetrate the forest shades, the muse encourages "the savage Youth" to sing about the heroism of his chiefs and about love. Wherever the muse of poetry comes, there one finds the ideas of glory, shame, integrity, and freedom.

The epode of the second ternary rehearses an appropriate but often repeated theme of the period: the movement of poetic genius from Greece northwest (see Pope's *Essay on Criticism,* Thomson's *Liberty,* Goldsmith's *Traveller,* etc.).[12] The first seven lines of the stanza evoke melodious names of places famous in Greek poetry and typical images of nature in it; and they argue that pain, not poetry, now emanates from them. It is curious and interesting that the idea has precedent in Milton's "On the Morning of Christ's Nativity," where Milton is delighted by the destruction of pagan influences through the coming of the new religion. Gray, by contrast, is sensitive only to the aesthetic havoc. Every bit of nature gave forth poetic music, the stanza continues, until, at the defeat of Greek independence by the Romans, the muses left their hill for the Roman territory. After Italy lost its freedom and independence during the Renaissance, the muses, who cannot live with tyranny, sought England's coast.

The first stanza of the third ternary is devoted wholly to Shakespeare, who is described as the favorite child of Nature (universal creation, including human nature, moral and physical laws, and so on). She showed herself to him, and he reached out for her; she gave him the pencil with which to describe the lesser nature (the appearance of the countryside, etc.); she gave him also the "golden keys" to the human emotions—one for comedy, the other for tragedy. Milton, who opens the second stanza of this group, is asserted to be equal with Shakespeare, in a phrase that echoes Milton's manner, "Nor second He." The first six lines of this antistrophe allude to the magnificence of his aim and execution in *Paradise Lost;* the next two, to his blindness, which Gray says came because in his poetic imagination he saw more divine truth, more of the throne of God, than a mortal could bear. The last four lines describe Dryden's sonorous achievement with the heroic couplet (the verse unit of two rhyming lines of iambic pentameter): the "Two Coursers of ethereal race," as Gray notes, are "Meant to express the stately march and sounding energy of Dryden's rhimes."

The opening five lines of the last stanza continue the praise of Dryden, who, as Gray goes on to say, was the last to attempt the "Æolian lyre," the noble and winged eloquence inherited from Pindar. Gray comments, in a note, that "We have had in our language no other odes of the sublime kind, than that of Dryden on St. Cecilia's day: for Cowley (who had his merit) yet wanted judgment, style, and harmony, for such a task. That of Pope is not worthy of so great a man. Mr. Mason indeed of late has touched the true chords, and with a masterly hand, in some of his Choruses. . . ." Cold though Gray may have been in his contact with strangers, putting Mason in this company shows that he could be positively torrid to a friend. Though Mason's poetry has long stopped breathing, he at least won a stay of mortality in a footnote.

The lyre, which Gray next addresses as he addressed it in the opening of the poem, is now being tried by a "daring Spirit"—Gray himself. He admits lacking both the pride—in this case the sense not of domineering vainglory, but of self-assurance and nobility—and the scope of Pindar, but he has been admitted to a share in the gift of imagination:

> Yet oft before his infant eyes would run
> Such forms, as glitter in the Muse's ray
> With orient hues, unborrow'd of the Sun.

He will try to "mount"—rise above the earth, in an allusion to the image of Pindar as an eagle—and he hopes to soar beyond the ordinary course of life. As a poet he will still be inferior to "the Good" (pious and virtuous people), but "far above the Great" (powerful ones).

The overall structure of the poem is clear, though the objections to its lack of essential solidity, beginning with Gray's own doubts and continuing through our time (as in Hagstrum's work), may well be valid. At the outset, Gray makes a general statement about the powers of lyric poetry, particularly of the sort that reaches as far as possible into the imagination, to arouse human emotions, calm them, and give a grace and meaning to life. The second ternary states the thesis that lyric poetry counterbalances the ills of life, that it is everywhere available where freedom and honor are, and that it successively left Greece and Rome when their people became enslaved and took up its domain in a free Britain. The third celebrates the most imaginative English poets, Shakespeare, Milton, and Dryden, and proclaims Gray's eagerness to be in their company.

There is surely a general sort of connection here, with all the stages of the thought holding together rationally; but one is likely to have the impression that the connection is oblique. The first and second ternaries are related, and the second and third as well; but it appears that there is not the same train of thought common to both connections. That is, the first and third ternaries deal with the power, glory, and nobility of elevated poetry and poets; the second, with a somewhat tangential subject, poetry as a guide to mankind. The first two ternaries are tied by a view of the social consequences of the emotional appeal of poetry; the second and third, merely by the geographical movement of the spirit of poetry. It is never clear why the particular poets Gray chooses to celebrate at the end are conspicuous for their fulfilling the promises of the second ternary. We grant him Milton as a champion of political freedom, but what exactly did Shakespeare, Dryden, and Gray himself do to carry freedom and independence to mankind? The point then is not that the views are irrational or disjointed but that there is no organic unity, no *tout ensemble* in Gray's own phrase, to make the poem artistically coherent.

And one must of course agree with Johnson that the explicit thesis of the poem is inaccurate: "that Poetry and Virtue go always together is an opinion so pleasing that I can forgive him who resolves to think it true."[13] Though one may choose to say that poetry flourishes best in an atmosphere of freedom, even the great poetry that Gray most admired has, historically, accompanied tyranny and chaos too. Virgil and Horace were court favorites of the dictator Augustus. Dante, certainly a believer in freedom, did not wish it for his enemies in the chaotic Italian politics of the thirteenth and fourteenth centuries. Racine, France's great tragic poet and the model for Gray's one attempt to write drama, enjoyed the support of Louis XIV, who was hardly famous for tolerating opposition. Shakespeare and his contemporaries, in the most brilliant period of English poetry, were ruled by England's most effective autocrat; Dryden was an active propagandist for the cynical Charles II and the absolutist James II. These poets were not toadies but were genuinely committed to the causes they espoused as the best hopes against the chaos of life; but that they were all champions of political liberty is certainly not true.

The change in governing imagery from the first ternary to the others again shows Gray's difficulties with unifying the poem. In the first group, harmony (poetry) is embodied in the metaphor of a flow of water, which gracefully fertilizes and impetuously overwhelms (combining in the first stanza, as Hagstrum has noted, the parallel and sometimes contrasting functions of art in the eighteenth century—to be beautiful and to be sublime). In the next two ternaries, the guiding image is the old one of the sun, but it is used with precision, dignity, and even freshness. Stanza 2.1, specifically calls the "heav'nly Muse" of poetry the sun which dissipates the ills of mankind; in 2.2, however, *this* sun—Poetry—is shown to go where the other, the visible sun, cannot. The next step, an extremely subtle one which prepares for the superb ending, is to present Shakespeare as Nature's darling even though—or because—he was nurtured "Far from the sun and summer-gale." Shakespeare was then given the secrets of a Nature unrelated to the surface appearance of things. The description of Milton further develops this idea, for he has been blinded by seeing too much of the far stronger light of truth, a light that, again, has nothing to do with the sun that we can see. The final stanza then makes "Bright-eyed Fancy" the purveyor of poetic sight, and the image culminates in the true poet's seeing visions that are "in the Muse's ray" and are colored with light "unborrow'd of the Sun."

Characteristically, Gray has made the sun of the ideal world the same as poetic imagination, where by tradition—as in Plato, Dante, and Milton (all favorites of his)—it is the supreme good, or God. It is true that the last line pays the appropriate homage to the good as superior to the beautiful, but the change from vision to abstract reflection of a different sort makes the reflection appear tacked on. The very intensity and complexity of the sun image tends to flatten the discursive statement that follows it, as it also compounds the structural difficulties in the poem. While the concentration, in the last two thirds of the poem, on an image of the ultimate ideal as the beautiful is extremely revealing of the period and of Gray, it tends to make the poem lopsided. The water image, which dominated the first third, seems to have been abandoned for a better one, not fused with it.

These structural imperfections keep "The Progress of Poesy" from being a very great poem, but there are ways in which it is most successful. To begin with, Gray's undertaking was a huge one: he was attempting, in imitation of the Greek ode writers, to develop a massively complex verse form that required of him the very greatest technical ability. The ode was to have three strophes and three antistrophes, each of twelve lines in the same meter and rhyme scheme as the others, and three epodes, each of seventeen lines in one meter and rhyme scheme. The strophes and antistrophes involve a complicated arrangement of tetrameter, pentameter, and a final alexandrine; the epodes use these three kinds of lines and add a trimeter line for good measure. And in all of them, Gray suits one of the finest poetic senses of sound in English literature with just about all the kinds of poetic feet used in the language and most of the permissible variations. It is a triumph of variety within a strict form.

As an example of this variation, in the openings of the strophes and antistrophes he is able to use the same meter for the sudden shock that is to simulate rapture (the opening line of the poem), muted adoration (1.2), melancholy reflection (2.1), matter-of-fact statement (2.2; 3.1), and allusive illustration of Milton's inverted phrasing (3.2). For a quick view of what Gray can do in identical meter, compare the epode of the first ternary with that of the second. In one stanza, the tetrameters that dominate the opening are light and gay in the manner of Milton's "L'Allegro" (and include direct echoes from that poem, as in line 31). They lead into a languorous description, full of color and slow graceful music, of Venus, the generalized ideal of the "bloom of young Desire, and purple light of Love." In the second epode, the same tetrameters, characterized by opening trochees as before, begin with the long vowels and frequent liquids that Gray knew so well how to use to give a melodious slowness to the verse. But the passage goes on, in condensed personifications recalling the Eton College ode, to modulate into tones of satire and epic dignity as Gray surveys the fate of empires. Metrically he has performed a remarkable feat, one much more ambitious than was usual in the English Pindaric ode.

But Gray was attempting still more—to continue a reasoned argument, decked out in splendid language. The coherence of the argument on the rational level has been seen, but it remains to be noted that in this poem the diction is consistently "elevated" beyond the routine and, what is more significant considering the early works, beyond any hint of triteness or standardized poetic diction. Instead, Gray is concerned with dignity and with the rendering of the ideally generalized: Mars and Jove, for example, are not schoolboy learning, but shorthand for similar but distinct states of the soul.

With its faults, then, "The Progress of Poesy" is an extremely significant achievement as well as a distinguished work of art. It brings a careful sense of form to a genre that had expanded sloppily in any direction that the practitioner chose. It is an experiment—like all of Gray's poetry—by a master craftsman, that covers, within a carefully delineated form, a range of meters and moods unmatched since Milton. The music and diction never fail Gray, even when he cannot keep a grasp on the central vision.

Like most of Gray's other poems, "The Progress of Poesy" also embodies his view of himself. The underlying effect of the poem is to aggrandize poetry and poets, thereby echoing a theme as old as Pindar. But it is also peculiarly relevant to the prevailing concern of Gray, examining and justifying his own lonely position at a distance from the mass of mankind: a position now perhaps aggravated by the illness and death of his beloved mother. From this point of view the second ternary relates him to society, for it argues that it is individual people like himself who give meaning to the rest of humanity. As is usual with Gray, this key statement most clearly appears in the center of the poem. Again, as is usual with him, the language of the ending, which specifically refers to him, makes him a generalized ideal—of the aspirant toward poetry—and makes morality and art the bases on which he wants the respect of the world. He is to be justified by the good that his imaginings do for himself and mankind, not by an artificial ranking system—a prouder version of the epitaph to the "Elegy" and for that matter of the theme of much of his serious poetry.

"The Bard"

Everything that can be said about the formal craftsmanship of "The Progress of Poesy" can be repeated about its companion ode, except that there need be no apology for the lack of central organic unity. Furthermore, Gray has added to all the matter packed into the earlier work the impressive features of a dramatic situation and a carefully composed picture. It may also be pointed out that one of the complaints against the poem—that the prophecies are too obscure—is irrelevant. If one considers the two odes as a unit, then

"The Progress of Poesy" is a series of pictures illustrating a thesis, and "The Bard" is the idealized expression of the argument (as the stonecutter-poet of the "Epitaph" was an idealized example of the fate of talented humanity doomed to obscurity in the preceding "Elegy"). That is, "The Progress of Poesy" imagines our world as one where poetry accompanies and supports national freedom, with the poets the true patriotic leaders. "The Bard" shows an idealized example of such a leader in an idealized situation of danger to the nation.

"The Bard" was a troublesome poem to compose. To Gray's recurring difficulty—"my Inspiration is very apt to fail me before I come to a conclusion" (*C,* 2:462)—was added ill health. He wrote to his intimate friend Dr. Thomas Wharton: "I have not done a word more of *Bard,* having been in a very listless, unpleasant, & inutile state of Mind for this long while, for wch I shall beg you to prescribe me somewhat strengthning & agglutinant, lest it turn to a confirm'd Pthisis" (*C,* 1:442–43). At last, a famous harpist, the blind Welshman John Parry, performed at Cambridge; and he "it was, that has put Odikle in motion again, & with much exercise it has got a *tender Tail* grown, like Scroddles [a pet name for Mason] . . ." (*C,* 2:502). Though the ending of "The Bard" failed to satisfy some of his friends, it had finally come. Conceivably, the gathering militarism of the mid 1750s, culminating in war with France in 1756, may have put patriotic fire into Gray and helped his inspiration, though the connections so far made are tenuous.[14]

As with "The Progress of Poesy," it may be useful to explicate "The Bard" in detail, though aside from the historical allusions it offers less difficulty. Gray's introductory advertisement gives the necessary source of conflict in the poem: "The following Ode is founded on a Tradition current in Wales, that EDWARD the First, when he compleated the conquest of that country, ordered all the Bards, that fell into his hands, to be put to death." As W. Powell Jones pointed out, Gray was skeptical about the story of Edward's murdering the bards, which he had found in Thomas Carte's *History of England.*[15] In Gray's essay "Cambri," one of the preparatory studies for his literary history, he had written of Edward that "he is said to have hanged up all their Bards, because they encouraged the Nation to rebellion, but their works (we see), still remain, the Language (tho' decaying) still lives, & the art of their versification is known, and practised to this day among them."[16] For Gray's purposes, of course, the question of fact is meaningless. The poem is to be a picture not of a specific historical event but rather of a typical, idealized, and critical scene: the nationalistic poet, the embodiment of the urge toward liberty, face to face with the tyrant. The thesis, implied rather than stated, is the inevitable triumph of the spirit over material rule. The prophecies thus are to be seen as having only a coincidental connection with subsequent English history, for they are also the generalized visions of the future, ideal rather than real.

As the poem opens, on a craggy and dangerous mountain path, Edward and his army are suddenly confronted by the last remaining Welsh bard, who calls down ruin on them. This scene, presented in the first stanza of the first ternary, remains throughout—except that to it are added, for a substantial stretch, the chanting ghosts of the murdered bards. Although Johnson thought that Gray had merely exploited an easy, stale device in beginning abruptly,[17] the opening stanza is one of the most admired in English poetry:

> "Ruin seize thee, ruthless King!
> Confusion on thy banners wait,
> Tho' fann'd by Conquest's crimson wing
> They mock the air with idle state.
> Helm, nor Hauberk's twisted mail,
> Nor even thy virtues, Tyrant, shall avail
> To save thy secret soul from nightly fears,
> From Cambria's curse, from Cambria's tears!"
> Such were the sounds, that o'er the crested pride
> Of the first Edward scatter'd wild dismay,
> As down the steep of Snowdon's shaggy side
> He wound with toilsome march his long array.
> Stout Glo'ster stood aghast in speechless trance:
> To arms! cried Mortimer, and couch'd his quiv'ring lance.

The second edition of the poem has a good many notes supplied by Gray. Most of them refer to lines of other poets that he recalled borrowing but some offer additional historical information. In stanza 1.1, for example, Gray cites a line by Shakespeare and one by Dryden that he has echoed, explains what a hauberk was, identifies the particular Gloucester and Mortimer who were officers in Edward's army, and discusses Mt. Snowdon in a way that well illustrates the amount and kind of learning he had accumulated: "*Snowdon* was a name given by the Saxons to that mountainous tract, which the Welch themselves called *Craigian-eryri:* it included all the highlands of Caernarvonshire and Merionethshire, as far east as the river Conway. R. Hygden speaking of the castle of Conway built by King Edward the first, says, 'Ad ortum amnis Conway ad clivum montis Erery;' and Matthew of Westminster, (ad ann. 1283) 'Apud Aberconway ad pedes montis Snowdoniae fecit erigi castrum forte' " (*CP*, 208). Because of his irritation with readers of the first edition who had complained of obscurity, Gray deliberately tells succeeding readers more than they care to know about his references.

Stanza 1.2, describes the bard—so that he will represent the generalized poet-hero—in attitudes traditional of bereavement, and it gives his view of the conqueror's effect on the world. The oaks, the caves, and the rushing river demand revenge on Edward, whose slaughter of the bards is eliminating nature's appointed spokesmen. Very significant is the echo here of "The Progress of Poesy" (2.3) where Gray had listed the various sites in Greece from which no music came because the country had lost its freedom—a further indication that the second poem is a dramatic exposition of one theme in the first. To the description Gray adds a note that clearly shows his reliance on established pictorial effects: "The image [of the beard and hair] was taken from a well-known picture of Raphael, representing the Supreme Being in the vision of Ezekiel: there are two of these paintings (both believed original), one at Florence, the other at Paris." Hagstrum rightly argues that the whole poem is conceived in a manner similar to that of the image: like the heads in Renaissance Italian paintings, he says "The Bard" is an attempt at a concentrated type of greatness, "that 'grandeur of generality,' that sublimity of *la belle nature,* to which great neoclassic art has often aspired."[18]

The epode of the first ternary consists of the bard's lament for the deaths of his companion bards, in images and diction much affected by a combination of the idea of the sublime and Gray's studies of primitive Welsh and Gothic poetry. Toward the end of it, the bard stops weeping, since he sees them, a band of ghosts, sitting on nearby cliffs, eager to avenge their throttled land. They prepare to join with him in prophecy as they unroll the future of Edward's family. We may note the perhaps unconscious repetition of a conspicuous image from the "Elegy," where Knowledge did *not* unroll her page to the rustics. And if we follow Gray's view of

himself as it appears in different poems, we see that here, as in the "Elegy," his spokesman *is* offered the vision on the scroll of truth. More clearly than in the earlier poem, the image assures the spokesman-poet of the survival and triumph of virtue.

In the second ternary the chorus—made up of the original speaker and the ghosts of his fellow bards—prophesies the fates of the royal family from Edward to Richard III. The first four lines of its first stanza are incantatory, leading to the actual fates that are to be disclosed; and the death of Edward II, in which his wife Isabel ("She-Wolf of France") was implicated, offers scope to gory imagery. As retribution for her inhumanity, her son Edward III becomes the terror of France, her country.

The second stanza of the second ternary is an imagined dialogue, narrated with great pleasure by the bards, between Edward III, lying on his death bed, and an ironic respondent. No one is concerned for the dying king—whose most promising heir, Edward the Black Prince, is already dead—and the court has deserted him for the successor, Richard II. (Note, by the way, line 69, "The Swarm, that in thy noon-tide beam was born," which borrows material from a line in Gray's abandoned play "Agrippina" and echoes an image in the "Ode on the Spring." The fairly standard poetic conception of crowds, courtiers, and youths as insects seems to have impressed Gray with its permanent relevance.) The lines on Richard II in this stanza, 71–77, are among the most famous in the poem; they combine precision of statement with considerable complexity of tone—the balminess of the day and the freshness of the frisking crew of the ship concentrate an image of carefree youth, while fate's agent, the Whirlwind, quietly prepares for a dreadful meal. Here is a fresher and even more horrifying version of the Eton College ode, more horrifying because it is narrated with glee, not by a sympathetic watcher and participant but by vengeful enemies.

The epode to the second ternary presents an intentionally blurred recital of havoc to contrast with the vivid concentration of the strophe and antistrophe in this section. First is the picture, in six lines, of Richard II's being starved to death in the midst of the revelry that characterized his reign. The remainder consists of the violent chaos of the Wars of the Roses, of which the battle scenes are summarized in lines 83–86. Next come the political murders in the Tower of London ("The oldest part of that structure is vulgarly attributed to Julius Caesar," says Gray's note, as he continues to persecute the reader with information). The towers themselves are asked to spare the holy head of Henry VI because of his virtue, his wife's heroic struggle for him, and his father (Henry V), England's symbol of heroic rule. The bards delight in weaving the future, "the winding sheet of Edward's race," in mixing together the white and red roses to foretell the pointless bloodshed. Wallowing nearby, the boar Richard III richly epitomizes the vicious destructiveness of the period and the obscene, mindless violence to which Edward's character tends.

The third ternary restores us to the Bard himself and affirms his triumph, both symbolic and historical, over Edward and what he represents. After informing Edward that his wife will suddenly die, the ghosts of the brother bards leave, their work done. They have woven the destiny of his race to its culmination, the murderous and self-destructive boar Richard III. Despite the bard's pleas, his friends vanish in the sunset (in imagery that recalls the concluding brilliance of "The Progress of Poesy"); but as recompense, their "glitt'ring skirts unroll" a glorious prospect of the restoration of legitimate rule in England with the coming in of the Welsh line of Tudors (Henry VII, the first Tudor king of England, defeated Richard III at Bosworth). Gray's notes on the last two lines of this stanza provide the necessary historical information: on Arthur, "It was the common belief of the Welch nation, that King Arthur was still alive in Fairy-Land, and should return again to reign over Britain"; on the "genuine Kings," "Both Merlin and Taliessin had prophesied, that the Welch should regain their sovereignty over this island; which seemed to be accomplished in the House of Tudor."

The second stanza of this last ternary is devoted to Queen Elizabeth, the most illustrious of the Tudors, particularly from the point of view of a poet: "In the midst a Form divine." Music plays around her, rhapsody is everywhere, with the sublime emotion pictured as a singing bird waving its many-colored wings upwards. The Bard properly calls on Taliessin, the greatest of all his colleagues, to be delighted, since her reign fosters the revival of British poetry, the ultimate victory of the bards over the barbarism of military despots like Edward I. The rhapsodic music and song "breathe a soul to animate thy clay." The spirit of the bards is reborn.

The last stanza begins with a condensed summary of the glorious poets of Elizabeth's time and after: poetry, the bard tells the ghosts of his brothers, revives and again sings its proper subjects. First, a line echoes Spenser's purpose in the *Faerie Queene,* in which imagination forms a song about truth, war, and love; next, Shakespeare is again admired for animating grief, pain, and horror; Milton is again seen as bringing breezes from the Garden of Eden in *Paradise Lost;* and the "distant warblings," as Gray informs us in a note, are "The succession of Poets after Milton's time." In line 135, the bard suddenly turns from his visions to Edward, whom he calls foolish for thinking that the bloody cloud of war and tyranny has quenched the sun of poetry. Tomorrow the sun returns, "And warms the nations with redoubled ray." The bard has seen and said enough. Since he knows that the eventual victory is his and that Edward's material, selfish concerns are doomed to both a short term and bloody retribution, he plunges to his death in triumph, not defeat.

"The Bard" is evidently the most complex poetic undertaking of all of Gray's works, structurally and metrically. He unified it in a number of ways. As Hagstrum has pointed out, the poem is carefully concentrated within one single scene, and the last two lines of the poem, Hagstrum says,

> describe an action imposed, as it were, on a canvas. They animate a hitherto static figure and constitute a climax, not of narrative action, but of pageant and tableau. Our attention has been fixed on relatively motionless, though not of course *e*motionless, figures and objects—on the venerable poet standing on a rock, on the mountainside itself, on the red sky of the sunset. But now, in a stroke, the bard and the sun have disappeared. The impoverished world is left to darkness—to "endless night" and the sound of roaring waters. The last effect of the poem, which Gray intended to be his greatest . . . is thus to dissolve its own visual fabric and to leave not a rack behind. If this action possesses force, it is because of the plastic solidity of the forms that are now destroyed.[19]

The figures contrasted in Gray's grand picture are again ideal symbols rather than actors in a specific, local situation. Nameless, the bard is a generalized Welsh bard, not a particular one of them. Similarly, Edward has been provided by history to personify tyranny as the physical representative of selfish wishes toward dominance—in him Gray could also imagine the starting point of the long series of brutal and meaningless wars that constitute English medieval history.

But the poem is not merely the representation in words of a

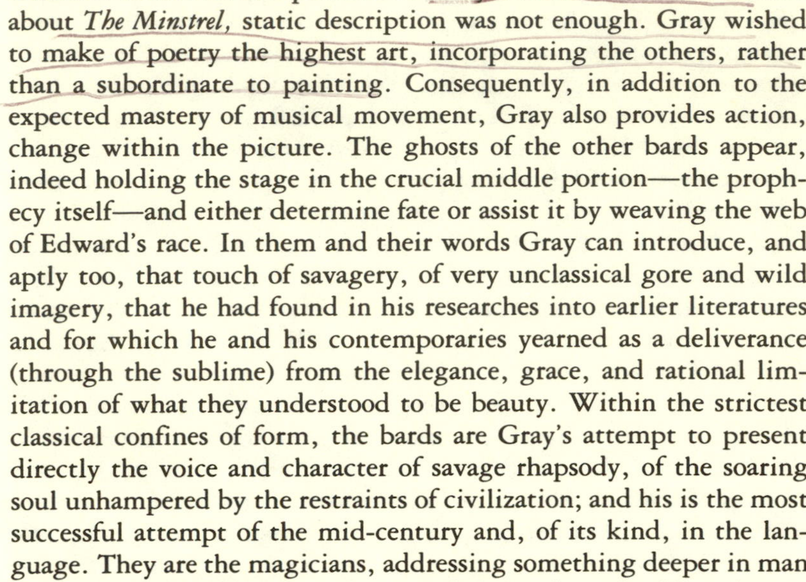

situation conceived as a picture. As Gray wrote to his friend Beattie about *The Minstrel,* static description was not enough. Gray wished to make of poetry the highest art, incorporating the others, rather than a subordinate to painting. Consequently, in addition to the expected mastery of musical movement, Gray also provides action, change within the picture. The ghosts of the other bards appear, indeed holding the stage in the crucial middle portion—the prophecy itself—and either determine fate or assist it by weaving the web of Edward's race. In them and their words Gray can introduce, and aptly too, that touch of savagery, of very unclassical gore and wild imagery, that he had found in his researches into earlier literatures and for which he and his contemporaries yearned as a deliverance (through the sublime) from the elegance, grace, and rational limitation of what they understood to be beauty. Within the strictest classical confines of form, the bards are Gray's attempt to present directly the voice and character of savage rhapsody, of the soaring soul unhampered by the restraints of civilization; and his is the most successful attempt of the mid-century and, of its kind, in the language. They are the magicians, addressing something deeper in man than the surface that fears death and fights for rule. They have a deep association with the underlying forces of nature—as witness their participation in the workings of destiny—and the assurance that their appeal to humanity is indestructible and will revive in spite of temporary repression.

Johnson's comment about the laxity of the end is valid on one level: "the ode might have been concluded with an action of better example; but suicide is always to be had without expense of thought."[20] It is true that deaths are the incompetent, lazy, or irresponsible writer's way out of plot difficulties, as innumerable weak novels and plays have shown. But here the objection overlooks both the plot, which makes the Bard's death inevitable, and the themes, which on the whole suggest suicide as the appropriate form of death. This conclusion—triumph and death—is a concentrated projection of Gray's steady preoccupations. Bereft of his friends, he can join them in death, meanwhile leaving the violence and irrationality of the world. Vindicated both by history and by high motives, the Bard wins over the world for altruistic reasons, heroically defending the enrichment of humanity. The end does not have the ambiguity of the "Elegy," though the suicide has struck some readers as abrupt and even ludicrous. Again, Gray's peculiar orientation may be responsible for this effect. Presumably if the Bard had rushed on to the ready spears of such as Mortimer (l. 14), readers like Johnson might be more satisfied. One would assume that such a thought had occurred to Gray in the months of reworking the poem and of worrying about ending it. Perhaps the simple and unaided suicide is a further indication of the Bard's, and Gray's, disdain for the multitude and of his superiority to its petty and selfish concerns. Perhaps it supports Roger Martin's analysis that Gray always yearned for a death without suffering, and therefore would reject the thought of the multitude of wounds entailed by a rush on the spears; and perhaps it is also the clearest symbolic union of Gray with the nature with which the Bard has earlier connected himself, as well as with the spirits of the past, who also emanate from nature.

Moral concerns, so important to Johnson, surely animate the poem, and for the first time in Gray they appear as drama—as the twentieth century prefers—rather than in discursive statement. The moral position simply affirms that the poetic element in mankind—by which Gray primarily means the yearning for elevation beyond matter, the sense of individual worth and individual integrity—is permanent and indestructible. Those elements seeking self-aggrandizement at the expense of others, and including insensibility to harmony and integrity, are vicious and lead to self-destructive impermanence. They are the clouds of evil lurking for man: the vulgar passions that destroy him (a preoccupation for Gray as early as the "Ode to Adversity" and the Eton College ode); the selfish wishes that alienate him from the rest of mankind, that prevent him from "knowing himself a man." The opposing poetic element is the sun, beaming upon and enriching man's life, forming a bond among all men and helping them to escape selfish and trivial aims. These were among Gray's most sincerely held convictions, and they express themselves clearly in the theme of "The Bard."

Underlying this poem, also, are Gray's most recurrent preoccupations, as Martin says and as we have seen them developing in the earlier writings and the letters. In "The Bard" we can see a projection of Gray—and we have his friend Norton Nicholls's evidence that Gray authorized this view—just as we see him in so many of his other poems, from the "Ode on the Spring" to the "Elegy." Here he is the representative of poetry, of the poet, face to face with the intrusive violence of selfish and domineering others—note that Edward I is not alone but at the head of an army, the crowd that threatens destruction if the chosen one does not change his ways. The self that Gray assumes, however, does not passively retreat, but instead holds his ground. He is sorrowful and forlorn, it is true; but, like Plato's philosophers, he is unswervingly courageous. The Bard also sees his old friends who, though dead, support him in his resistance to the tyranny of the crowd of vicious vulgar, an ideal arrangement for the man who yearns for elite company but resists incorporation into the swarm of humanity. The dead bards, aside from conveniently suggesting the prophecy of history (Gray's continuous study) against the tyrant and for the free human soul, also suggest the long tradition of poetry of which Gray had already twice seen himself as the current representative in his writings—covertly and modestly, as the Stonecutter-poet in the "Elegy," and overtly at the end of "The Progress of Poesy." If one insisted on going further, the ghosts no doubt owe a good deal to the long list of Gray's own dead, to whom he is steadily tending: by this time, the eleven brothers and sisters, the father, the intimate friend West, various uncles and aunts with whom he had been close, and most recently the beloved mother.

The versification of "The Bard" is even more ambitious than that in "The Progress of Poesy," the strophes and antistrophes being longer still. Gray incorporates both the imagery of Celtic and Gothic literature and, in meter and alliterative effects, its characteristic manner, while insisting on the strictest Greek form. As W. Powell Jones has noted, "The theme was sublime, Pindaric, and he made it savage besides, by bringing in the trochaic refrain of an Old Norse poem he had been reading, as well as a hint of the complicated *Gorchest-beirdh* from Welch prosody. A strict Pindaric ode on such a subject was new and startling. . . . "[21] The alliterative and heavily rhythmic effects are clearly derived from Gray's study of Welsh metrics, as various critics have shown and as his essay "Cambri" proves.[22] To this elaborate body of sources may be added the variety of classical and English poems that Lonsdale cites, all of which Gray fuses into an extraordinarily ambitious technical achievement.

Because of the dramatic design, the emotional changes in "The Bard" are even more powerful than the superb technical effects of "The Progress of Poesy." In stanza 3.1, for example, the simple but realized situation of the Bard when his ghostly friends leave involves, within the 14 lines, first the combination of ecstasy and matter-of-factness with which the ghosts bid farewell to the tyrant, then the pitiful forlornness of the Bard, then his shimmering view of their departure, then his awe as the future crowds upon him, and finally his rapture as he responds to the distant glories and triumphs. All this, of course, is in the same metrical scheme as the violent shock of the famous opening stanza. The whole work is played out in the wild hills of Wales, and Gray makes sure that we never forget the commanding Mt. Snowdon or the torrent rushing far below, the sun above and the "endless night" in the depths—the simple, elemental images that fit superbly the elemental feelings and thesis of the poem.

A word remains to be said about one complaint, which is indicated by H.J.C. Grierson in his comment that "the prophecy of the bard loses dramatic and convincing power by the neatness and accuracy of its historic detail."[23] The objection, more generally put, is that Gray's work, particularly the Pindaric Odes, is too obviously crafted. For many kinds of poetry, such a quality would constitute a damning flaw; it may well be that for "The Progress of Poesy" and "The Bard." But it must be pointed out that Gray used a genre, the regular Pindaric, that entails very conscious, visible care merely to fulfill its metrical requirements. Six very long stanzas of one sort, and three of another, each most complicated in rhyme and meter, cannot have identical patterns by happy inspiration alone. In his diction, Gray aims for novelty, dignity, precision, harmony, and color—some of them elements that cannot be chanced upon. Though there is real feeling behind the odes—the feeling generated by the mental preoccupations already noted—many readers have been unable themselves to feel, though they may admire, the desperately sought passion and wild fire. Even toward these ends, "The Bard" illustrates how far sensitivity, learning, and art can aspire.

Chapter Six
Minor Poems

"A Long Story"

All of Gray's poetry that makes claims on more than historical importance—that ranks as his best—has now been discussed. But while his production was very small considering his leisure and his lifelong devotion to literature, he did begin a fair number of other poems and even finished a few. Four complete poems, a fragment, and a satiric trifle were published in Gray's lifetime in addition to those poems so far dealt with. Because of his special artistic involvement and skill, they are always interesting, if not always successful.

Of these, the first was "A Long Story," a series of comic verses occasioned by the visit of Miss Henrietta Speed and Lady Schaub to Gray's residence during his summer vacation in 1750. They were guests of Lady Cobham at her manor at Stroke Poges, and the purpose of their visit was to invite the poet to meet their hostess. Gray was out when they called, but he returned the visit, and the ladies and he subsequently became good friends.

Gray found in them good nature, vivacity, and some degree of maternal solicitude, while they had in him wit, poetic fame, and kind concern. Though the three were of course not constant companions, they did become so close that Gray was to help Miss Speed attend Lady Cobham in her last illness ten years later. The poem therefore has considerable biographical interest, both in its reflection of Gray's view of himself and in its consequences. Among the consequences were strong indications that Lady Cobham was interested in arranging a match between Gray and Miss Speed (a considerable heiress), who does not seem to have been averse to the idea. Gray was not interested in marriage, and the lady eventually, at the age of about forty, married the Comte de Viry, a Savoyan nobleman considerably her junior. (*C*, 1:331, n. 1).

Two letters from Miss Speed to Gray give glimpses of their friendship, probably as close a one as Gray could have with an eligible single woman. The first, a short note, indicates how she and Lady Cobham were delighted with "A Long Story." The other cautions him about the unhealthiness of staying in London in August: "now I know you are insensible to heat or cold, not but that your Body suffers by either extreme, but you have not attention enough to yourself to seek a remedy" (*C*, 2:637). Later in Gray's life he was still enjoying the company of Miss Speed and her friends, but with an amused exasperation aroused by their lack of intellectuality: "I have pass'd a part of the summer on a charming hill near Henley with the Thames running at my foot; but in the company of a pack of Women, that wore my spirits, tho' not their own. the rest of the season I was at Cambridge in a duller, & more congenial, situation" (*C*, 2:703).

The relevance of "A Long Story" to Gray's view of himself as against the rest of the word has been best discussed by Roger Martin, who says that it translates into images the success of the "Elegy." It thus represents the homage from outside, the fears of the secret self, the shame at being seen, the mockery, and the self-doubt. It also shows, according to Martin, Gray's imagination delighting in conceiving the facets of his triumph in the feminine hurly-burly, as well as his justification as a poet before a fair court.[1] This analysis seems quite sound, except that the initial spur cannot be specifically the great success of the "Elegy." The "Elegy" was not published until February 1751, though it had been finished by June 1750; "A Long Story" seem to have been written in late summer and early fall of 1750. The motivation for the pride would then be a sense of achievement and of anticipated triumph, perhaps fed by the high praise of those friends to whom Gray had shown or given copies of his masterpiece.

Allowing for the cheerier world of comedy, the two women in "A Long Story" seem as grossly and irrationally violent as Edward I on a bard hunt:

> The trembling family they daunt
> They flirt, they sing, they laugh, they tattle,
> Rummage his Mother, pinch his Aunt,
> And up stairs in a whirlwind rattle.

"Each hole and cupboard they explore"—they look into everything in his private rooms hoping to find him. They appear to pose no threat except to his privacy, but, in a passage that begs every modern reader to throttle the Freud within him, they do wear armor hidden under their bonnets, aprons, and capucines. Gray's spokesman in the poem does not hide his sense of annoyance and fear at this invasion by the outside world, though he does regard these fears ironically. At the center of the poem, the Poet is spirited away by his protectors, the Muses: a symbolic version of his detachment from vulgar life through his dedication to poetry, which a Freudian would be likely to see as an Oedipal reliance on his mother. "Underneath their hoops," they take him to a place where, in a caricature of the narrator of "Ode on the Spring" and the "Elegy," "safe and laughing in his sleeve, / He heard the distant din of war." The "spell" that they left on the table, the note inviting him to call at the castle, again suggests the attraction that the world had for him, an attraction that he found himself unable to resist.

At Lady Cobham's he is tried for his magic, which he defends as being white, not black. He is attacked by the ghosts of ladies, descended from their portraits on the walls, who are shocked to see a commoner received in the impressive castle that he had described in the first four stanzas. Mason's comment on the similarity of this technique to that in "The Bard" helps point to the strength of Gray's sense of being on trial, particularly by the past: "Here Fancy is again uppermost, and soars as high on her comic, as on another occasion she does on her lyric wing: For now a chorus of ghostly old women of quality come to give sentence on the culprit Poet, just as the spirits of Cadwallo, Urien, and Hoel join the Bard in dreadful symphony to denounce the vengeance on Edward I. The route of Fancy, we see, is the same both on the humorous and sublime occasion. No wonder, therefore, if either of them should fail of being generally tasted."[2] History, in "A Long Story," attacks Gray in contrast to its support of the Bard in the later poem; but, in the context of Gray's mind, history's stress on aristocratic greatness has been neatly dissipated in the contemporaneous "Elegy." To the shock of all these jurors, Lady Cobham graciously receives him with an invitation to dinner; Gray triumphs over class barriers, mingling with the "great" as Swift, a scribbler advanced to even higher society, had shown himself in such poems as "The Author upon Himself" (1714). But Gray's triumph is ironically minimized by the suggestion at the end that Lady Cobham wastes her time indiscriminately: after the presumed gap of five hundred stanzas, Gray concludes,

> And so God save our noble King,
> And guard us from long-winded Lubbers,
> That to eternity would sing,
> And keep my Lady from her Rubbers.

Analyzing the underlying psychological movement, then, tends to reveal Gray's orientation to the rest of mankind more clearly than in his major poems, since he is off guard in "A Long Story." But a man's psychological stance consists not only of the unguarded response (for his thinking is presumably characteristic too), and consequently that alone misrepresents him. And the bare configuration of his responses is merely the material or shape of the way the work of art is to be, not the work itself. Any ordinary person may have a similar view of himself in relation to society, but he cannot make of it poetry. Put another way, "A Long Story," so private to Gray, is more symbolic case history than poetry.

Its critical reception has been on the whole unfavorable. Gray himself decided not to reprint it in the 1768 edition of his poems because it was not the public's business, which would imply that he had not universalized it into art. As he wrote to Beattie in December 1767, he had allowed Dodsley to print it in the 1753 edition only for the sake of Bentley's design (*C*, 3:982). And indeed, as Walpole's explanation of the Frontispiece suggests, that picture is a playful delight: "The Muses conveying the Poet under their hoops to a small closet in the garden. Fame in the shape of Mr. P——is flying before; and after him the two female warriors as described in the verses. On one side is my lord keeper Hatton dancing; and among the ornaments are the heads of the Pope and queen Elizabeth nodding at one another; behind him is a papal bull, a phial of sublimate, a dagger and a crucifix; behind her the cannon called queen Elizabeth's pocket-pistol."

Johnson dismissed the poem with a line in the biographical section of his "Life of Gray" and did not deign to consider it in the critical part: "An invitation from Lady Cobham about this time gave occasion to an odd composition called *A Long Story*, which adds little to Gray's character."[3] When we consider, for example, the nobility and wit of Swift's occasional poems to Stella, or the rollicking spirits and plain social joy of Goldsmith's pieces to his friends, we can hardly quarrel with Johnson here. "A Long Story" is, at best, a harmless though revealing set of verses, a weak specimen of a minor mode.

Translations from the Norse and Celtic

Far more important than the other poems treated in this chapter, both intrinsically as works of art and historically as indications of literary trends, are the two Norse "odes" and the Welsh "fragment" that Gray gave to Dodsley to substitute for "A Long Story" in the 1768 edition of his works. According to W. Powell Jones's invaluable book on Gray's scholarly activities, "By 1755, if we may judge from his pocket notebooks for that year, he was well under way in his thorough study of poetics—Romance, Germanic, and Celtic—as a background for the historical origins of English prosody. By 1758 he had practically abandoned the study of poetics for English antiquities, but meanwhile he had written articles in his Commonplace Book on early English poetry, on Welsh lore, and on things Norse that mark him as a genuine English pioneer in those fields."[4] Gray's Advertisement to the poems confirms this evidence from his note books: "The Author once had thoughts (in concert with a Friend) of giving *the History of English Poetry:* In the Introduction to it he meant to have produced some specimens of the Style that reigned in ancient times among the neighbouring nations, or those who had subdued the greater part of this Island, and were our Progenitors: the following three Imitations made a part of them"(*CP*, 27).

These poems are, then, the direct result of Gray's fascination with the Gothic, which by this time was becoming fashionable, partly because of the fame of "The Bard." Bishop Percy was currently collecting material for his *Reliques of Ancient English Poetry,* showing a great though amateur interest in the primitive elements of literature. Macpherson, very likely inspired to his counterfeits by "The Bard" (among other stimuli), was producing the bardic literature of the highlands that made Gray so enthusiastic. Others in the 1760s—notably Laurence Sterne, Charles Churchill, and later Thomas Chatterton—were actively subverting whatever neoclassical standards of elegance successful novelists like Defoe, Richardson, Smollett, and even Fielding had left. (Fielding, the great exemplar of that elegance in fiction before Jane Austen, was giving it up in *Amelia* around 1750.) William Collins, the only contemporary lyricist comparable to Gray, had years before worked on an unfinished manuscript, an "Ode on the Superstitions of the Highlands of Scotland" that embodied the mid-century's interest in the irrational and the fantastic. Gray, however, was the only poet of note to feel his way into the barbaric directness of Gothic poetry; and he was the only one to attempt to reproduce it in English in imagery, diction, tone, and meter. Even Johnson, uneasy though he was made by experiment and innovation, grudgingly admitted the worth of these poems: "His translations of Northern and Welsh Poetry deserve praise; the imagery is preserved, perhaps often improved; but the language," he adds for the sake of consistency, "is unlike the language of other poets."[5]

The first of Gray's translations (written in 1761) was printed as "The Fatal Sisters. An Ode (From the Norse Tongue) in the Orcades of Thormodus Torfaeus . . . and also in Bartholinus"—note Gray's scrupulous citation of his sources. According to the *Complete Poems* (211), this ode is based on an Icelandic poem of the eleventh century originally untitled but later named *Darrathor Lioth,* which means either "Lay of the Dart" or "The Song of Darrathor." The scene is the Battle of Clontarf, which was fought on Good Friday 1014. Gray does not seem to have known Old Norse well enough to work directly from that language. Rather, he probably used the literal translations into Latin in Bartholin's book, piecing out the sense of the Norse with its help. As with his Welsh studies, which are embodied in his article "Cambri," he could easily have deduced the special metrical qualities of the originals without knowing the language well.[6]

Gray's preface gives the circumstances necessary to understand the poem (though he mistakes the holiday): "on Christmas-day (the day of the battle,) a Native of *Caithness* in Scotland saw at a distance a number of persons on horseback riding full speed towards a hill, & seeming to enter into it . . . looking thro' an opening in the rocks he saw twelve gigantic figures resembling Women: they were all employ'd about a loom; & as they wove, they sung the following dreadful song; wch when they had finish'd, they tore the web into twelve pieces & (each taking her portion) gallop'd six to the North & as many to the South" (*CP*, 27–28). The Valkyrie, the "Fatal

Sisters" of the title who speak in chorus throughout the poem, are accurately defined in Gray's notes as "female Divinities, Servants of *Odin* (or *Woden*) in the Gothic mythology: their name signifies *Chuser{s} of the slain.* they were mounted on swift horses with drawn swords in their hands, & in the throng of battle selected such as were destined to slaughter, & conducted them to *Valhalla,* the hall of *Odin,* or paradise of the Brave, where they attended the banquet, & served the departed Heroes with horns of mead and ale" (*CP*, 214).

Their actions seem to touch something basic in Gray. Like the bards of the greater, original poem of four years before, they are engaged in weaving fate with a bloody material—in this case "human entrails"—and using human heads, spears, and swords as the instruments of weaving. Gray catches and amplifies the exulting violence of Gothic battle songs, the sense of elemental amorality of the divinities, their delight in the appurtenances of a battlefield—clashing weapons, blood, bleakness, corpses everywhere—exactly in the spirit of such surviving Anglo-Saxon war poems as the "Battle of Maldon" or the "Battle of Brunanburh." He has reached beyond the Olympian gods of his older sources to something that appeals to him as deeper than reason. He has sought out and found an element existing also in pre-Olympian Greek mythology, in the furies and horrifying local demons that we now see in the background of classical antiquity but that would not have been prominent in the eighteenth-century view of that era. Gray's imitation projects the compulsion toward horror that the earlier eighteenth century chose to ignore as primitive but that is conspicuous in Norse poetry and, as the events of the twentieth so bitterly attest, eternal in man.

"The Fatal Sisters" also brilliantly echoes the verse form and the language of the Northern poetry. Though Gray concedes to his time and to convention the rhyme that he believed they required, and though he uses a recognizable English meter, trochaic tetrameter, he does approximate the four-stress effect of the Gothic by binding together key lines with powerful alliterations: '*H*aste, the loom of *H*ell prepare," 'Glitt'ring *l*ances are the *l*oom," etc. A line of trochaic tetrameter has, of course, four stressed syllables, but each is normally followed by one unstressed syllable, and the caesura (the main pause) can come almost anywhere in the line. In Anglo-Saxon practice there was no regular restriction on the number or places of the unstressed syllables, and the four heavy stresses were normally evenly divided by the caesura. Milton's "Hail, divinest Melancholy" is an example of a line of regular trochaic tetrameter. As a deliberate contrast, in such a line as "Iron-sleet of arrowy shower" Gray balances two unaccompanied strongly stressed syllables with two others that carry along four unstressed ones. Again in keeping with the older style, instead of the personifications and the generalized diction in which Gray had earlier indulged—often so triumphantly as to justify the theory of poetry that made them conspicuous—he now presents concrete, specific diction of the simple sort that Wordsworth was to advocate in the preface to the *Lyrical Ballads.*

The second of these translations, "The Descent of Odin, an Ode," also—as Gray notes on the title page—comes from Bartholin's book. According to the *Complete Poems* (216), its source was the Icelandic "*Vegtamskvitha* ('The Ballad of Vegtam,' a name meaning 'Traveller' assumed by Odin in the poem)." In this poem Gray seeks a primitive kind of grandeur and an air of weirdness rather than the wild blood-lust in the other imitation. Consequently, the diction is more restrained; the alliteration less pronounced; in general, the tone more civilized. However, the lines still have the incantatory heavy four-foot beat, and the language is far simpler than in Gray's original poetry.

Significantly, Gray chose one of his favorite themes for translation: the return of someone from the dead, in this instance a repulsive giantess. She prophesies, as did the poets of the Eton College ode and "The Bard." If we wish to extend the suggestions of this theme, we can even see in Odin's visit the coming of dangerous authority (like that of Edward I); this powerful representative of the outer world threatens the Prophetess Giant-Mother, who wants complete withdrawal from that world, without even the longing, lingering look back of the "Elegy." She predicts Doomsday, that same *Götterdämmerung* that Wagner was to elaborate from the same mythology; and she will not rise from sleep until Night has resumed its rule: "Till wrap'd in flames, in ruin hurl'd, / Sinks the fabrick of the world." Is this again an echo of "The Bard," a kind of satisfaction for Gray both in his own defiance of grandeur and in destruction, of himself as well as of the obtrusive and dangerous outside? If "The Descent of Odin" had been original with him, we would be justified in indulging a train of thought not absolutely valid for an imitation.

But we can fairly argue that Gray was seduced into translating this poem, and not another, because it reflected some of his continuing concerns.

"The Triumphs of Owen. A Fragment," based on a Latin translation of a twelfth-century Welsh poem by Gwalchmai, is less impressive than the Norse pieces, perhaps because, as the title indicates, Gray never finished reworking it to his satisfaction. The language, close to that of the genteel side of the eighteenth century, seems inappropriate to harsh and elemental battle. Even in the first stanza the conventional weighs down the spirit, beginning with the third line, "Fairest flower of Roderic's stem," and the last four lines of the poem suffer from routine personifications:

> There Confusion, Terror's child,
> Conflict fierce, and Ruin wild,
> Agony, that pants for breath,
> Despair and honourable Death.

The meter seems more to rock than—as in the Norse imitations—to arrest by a slow, heavy beat. In general, "The Triumphs of Owen" can easily strike a modern reader as an exercise, not an emotional recapturing of the spirit of another society. Indeed, he apparently rejected a heroic, violent conclusion in the original: according to Richard Bridgman, "he substituted a melodramatic litany of terror, confusion, ruin, agony, and despair for one of glorification, then stopped on an honorable death, without, it should be said, feeling any obligation to include reference to the prolonged uncertainty of God's judgment yet to come."[7]

Gray's Gothic poems, as critics have observed, open new avenues for poetic exploration in subject, in technique, and in psychological aim. Passing beyond the artificial simulation of wildness for which various writers on "the sublime" offered recipes, the most successful of these poems—"The Fatal Sisters"—seems to go directly to basic, elemental responses to life of the sort found, for example, in the Old Testament "Song of Deborah," in the choruses of the Greek tragedian Aeschylus, and in Indian and African chants. If, as Roger Martin argues, the poet sought all of his days to vanish from life, then he here succeeded in losing himself in the generalized unconscious of wild, raw instinct—just as the self-tormenting ego of the twentieth century can lose itself in proliferating brutal mass religions. In any event, the rapture of drowning oneself in instinctual, generalized human emotion is yet another solution to Gray's problem of relating himself to humanity at large.

"On Lord Holland's Seat Near Margate"

The poem on Holland's seaside estate, written in 1768, was published anonymously in 1769 without Gray's permission. A violently partisan attack on a repellent politician, its language is, as is usual with Gray, effectively precise. Lord Holland has chosen to retire to a desolate spot on the seacoast since he is now "Old and abandon'd by each venal friend." Regarded as a destroyer in every act of his life, he aggravates the desolation of local nature by building Gothic ruins everywhere; and he muses that, if his political friends had been true, he might have achieved the destruction of London by war and fire:

> Far other scenes than these had bless'd our view
> And realis'd the ruins that we feign.
> Purg'd by the sword and beautifyed by fire,
> Then had we seen proud London's hated walls,
> Owls might have hooted in St. Peters Quire,
> And foxes stunk and litter'd in St. Pauls.

Though the poem's object means nothing to us now, we may still find the bitter wit entertaining; but when David Cecil considers these lines evidence "that, had he chosen, Gray could . . . have rivalled Pope as a satirist in the grand manner,"[8] he exceeds the license Oxbridge dons have for mutual admiration. Since Gray never chose to write satire for an audience more extensive than a few close friends, he evidently could not have dared the grand, open attack on power that Pope, Swift, or Gray's younger contemporary Churchill enjoyed. Language, of course, means a great deal in any sort of poetry, including satire; but language alone is not enough, and that is the case here. What vision of life large enough for grand satire animates this picture of an old, isolated, defeated minister yearning for destruction? If we compare it even with the sonnet to West we can see how narrow its focus is. It is a trifle, and Gray was right to resent its publication.

"Ode for Music"

Gray was contemptuous of all poetry written to order for a ceremonial occasion, referring to "state-poems" as "my ancient aversion" (*C*, 1:295). He had, after all, rejected the poet laureateship because he could not conceive of decently writing poetry to suit someone else's desire for aggrandizement. Once, however, he found himself obliged to write such a poem, the "Ode for Music," for the installation of the duke of Grafton as chancellor of Cambridge University on 1 July 1769. Grafton had appointed Gray Regius Professor of Modern History at Cambridge the year before, and it was no more than common gratitude, to say nothing of sound politics, for Gray to offer to write the ode even before he was asked. He would have preferred the verses to appear without his name, for as he wrote to Beattie, "I do not think them worth sending you, because they are by nature doom'd to live but a single day, or if their existence is prolong'd beyond that date, it is only by means of news-paper parodies, & witless criticism" (*C*, 3:1070.).

Critical comment on the poem has been at best tolerant. Edmund Gosse, for example, says that is has beautiful passages but is on the whole inferior: "In it he returns, with excess, to that allegorical style of his youth from which he had almost escaped, and we are told a great deal too much about 'painted flattery' and 'creeping Gain,' and visionary gentlefolks of that kind." Elwin, the reviewer of Mitford's edition of Gray's correspondence, was surprisingly charitable: "though the 'Ode for Music' is not equal to 'The Bard,' or 'The Progress of Poetry,' it is better than any other that was ever composed for a kindred purpose"—a view that, considering only such works as spring to mind as the topical poems of Dryden or Spenser or Jonson or Donne, is pure nonsense. Martin is more just and less kind; he considers the poem mediocre because of the contrast between the grandeur of the design and the absence of conviction.[9] But the "Ode for Music" does show much of Gray's old skill with language, though we can understand Coleridge's objection that the personifications are mere abstractions. At any rate, we are faced with them right away. The first stanza, or "Air," forbids the "holy ground" of Cambridge to the reveler Comus and his crew, and to Ignorance, Sloth, Sedition, Servitude, and Flattery. The next, "Chorus," also sends both Envy and Gain away from Cambridge, the seat of the muses and of bright-eyed Science.

The "Recitative" that follows is much fresher and more attractive: the poet says that he has heard the foregoing prohibitons bursting from the sky above, where are "the sainted Sage, the Bard divine"—Newton and Milton, the twin glories of Cambridge. They are among the chosen few (the steady objects of Gray's fellow feeling): "the Few, whom Genius gave to shine / Through every unborn age, and undiscovered clime." Though "Rapt in celestial transport," Newton and Milton kindly glance at their old university from time to time, "To bless the place, where on their opening soul / First the genuine ardor stole."

The "Air" that follows is presumably sung by Milton, while Newton listens and nods approval. As a minor indication of Gray's versatility, this "Air" duplicates the very complicated stanza of Milton's "On the Morning of Christ's Nativity," except that pentameter replaces the original tetrameter of the next-to-last line. The sense of the stanza is that Milton had often strolled on the Cambridge lawns at dawn, had observed the lingering Cam river, and had contemplated the moon in dim cloisters—in many ways a reflection both of Milton's melancholy man in "Il Penseroso" and of the image of Gray that appears so often in his early poetry and that presumably remained available for poetic exploitation.

As in "A Long Story" and "The Bard," the ghostly past manifests itself, here through a procession of noble and royal benefactors of Cambridge. Inevitably, Gray also echoes the "Elegy":

> (Their tears, their little triumphs o'er,
> Their human passions now no more,
> Save Charity, that glows beyond the tomb.)

In the symbolic permanence of charity, Gray unites the wish that he so movingly expressed in the "Elegy" for leaving some sign of oneself behind with his insistence that virtue and maturity consist in feeling for others. The following "Quartetto" is the song of these noble benefactors, which they begin by concentrating in two pithy lines the justification of aristocracy, the code of Plato's guardians in the Republic: "What is Grandeur, what is Power? / Heavier toil, superior pain." The only reward is " 'The grateful mem'ry of the Good,' " again a very strong echo of the "Elegy" and of Gray's own wishes that had been expressed so often in his letters and occasionally—most recently in "The Progress of Poesy"—in his poems.

In the next "Recitative" Margaret of Anjou welcomes Grafton; in the "Air" that follows, she continues to praise him, in a direct recollection (perhaps unsuspected by Gray) of two of the central stanzas of the "Elegy," at least two of the most disputed:

Thy liberal heart, thy judging eye,
The flower unheeded shall descry,
And bid it round heaven's altars shed
The fragrance of it's blushing head:
Shall raise from earth the latent gem
To glitter on the diadem.

These lines are evidence, if any were needed, that in the greater poem Gray had regretted the wasting of the flower and of the gem and that he could identify himself with both. Margaret continues in the subsequent recitative to praise both Cambridge and Grafton: Cambridge modestly gives Grafton the rule, "While Spirits blest above and Men below / "Join with glad voice the loud symphonious lay." The Grand Chorus that ends the poem assures us that Grafton will guide the ship of Cambridge honorably and watchfully, while "The Star of *Brunswick* smiles serene, / And gilds the horrors of the deep." If we compare this fatuous prophecy with that of the bards in the earlier poem, we see how little this poem mattered to Gray.

The "Ode for Music," to summarize, is a competent fulfillment of a debt of gratitude. In occasional passages, where it touches Gray's deepest underlying feelings, it achieves the dignified tenderness that everywhere pervades the "Elegy." Otherwise, it is a mélange of his old themes, worked together but not integrated. By using the "irregular ode" form (in contrast with the regular Pindarics of 1757), Gray showed that he was settling for loose development. None of the stanzas in this form is symmetrically related to the others either by a clear organization into triads or by perceptible recollections of metrical patterns. It is a good exercise, but the man who had written the Eton Ode, the "Elegy," and the Pindaric Odes had little reason to be prouder of it than he was.

Posthumous Poems, Fragments, Trivia

"Agrippina, a Fragment of a Tragedy." Besides those poems so far discussed, Gray worked on several others that he did not finish. He began "Agrippina" in the winter of 1741–42 and, in the judgment of all his critics but Mason, he did well to abandon it not longer after. While working on it, he wrote wryly of its lack of form: "I fancy, if it ever be finished, it will be in the nature of Nat. Lee's Bedlam Tragedy, which had twenty-five acts and some odd scenes" (*C*, 1:189). Four years later he sent a scene from the play to Walpole, commenting that "if it don't make you cry, it will make you laugh; and so it moves some passion, that I take to be enough" (*C*, 1:258). Furthermore he complains that the fragment (which he had come upon while rummaging through old papers) has speeches "all in figures and mere poetry, instead of nature and the language of real passion" (*C*, 1:262). When we add to this judgment by the author the fact that Mason, who first printed the fragment, admitted to making changes in the assignment of speeches—changes that cannot be identified[10]—then we can be sure that "Agrippina" has few claims as a work of literature. Even in its failure, however, it can tell us something about Gray as man and as poet.

Mason furnished a long plan of the complex events intended for this play that centers on the character of the mother of Nero. The 194 surviving lines never go beyond the first sentence of this "Argument": "The drama opens with the indignation of Agrippina at receiving her son's orders from Anicetus to remove from Baiae, and to have her guard taken from her,"[11] but it is elaborate rather than fiery. As every commentator on the fragment has pointed out, the length of the heroine's speeches destroys whatever dramatic effect might have inhered in the subject. Whether Gray might have learned to write plays is a purely academic issue, since he never again tried to do so. Perhaps he became aware that his talent lay not in feeling himself into a variety of individual responses to the world but rather in generalizing his own limited responses through the medium of lyric poetry.

However, the themes of "Agrippina" are worth touching upon. The subject is the relationship between a dominating mother and an ambitious, imperious, and vicious son. While Gray's own mother was his conscious idol, she must have been a strong-minded woman to endure her very bitter life both as a mother (eleven of her twelve children died in infancy or at birth) and as the wife of a brutal and irresponsible neurotic. Though Gray loved and revered her, it would seem natural that he also, at least at this early stage of his life, would have had some underlying resentment against her very strength and goodness. He probably felt guilty about having no prospects through which to repay her expectations of his future, whether or not she expressed any. Finishing his legal studies despite his dislike of both the subject and his fellow students, and despairing about ever doing anything worthwhile imply an awareness of obligation and insufficiency on his part, presumably with respect to his mother. At the same time, the fragment immediately precedes the creative period of the spring and summer of 1742, in which a major theme was the attempt of the young poet to achieve for himself a measure of independence and a livable relationship with the rest of humanity. In Agrippina's complaint we can see an imagined response to the attempt to cut the umbilical cord. She tells her "Confidant" Aceronia that Nero was raised to power only by her, that the boy had himself not known what his relations to the rest of the world were to be until she showed him:

> 'Tis like, thou hast forgot, when yet a stranger
> To adoration, to the grateful steam
> Of flattery's incense, and obsequious vows
> From voluntary realms, a puny boy,
> Deck'd with no other lustre, than the blood
> Of Agrippina's race, he liv'd unknown
> To fame, or fortune; haply eyed at distance
> Some edileship, ambitious of the power
> To judge of weights and measures; scarcely dar'd
> On expectation's strongest wing to soar
> High as the consulate, that empty shade
> Of long-forgotten liberty: When I
> Oped his young eye to bear the blaze of greatness;
> Shew'd him, where empire tower'd, and bad[e] him strike
> The noble quarry.

Reminded of Nero's power, she looses another blast against him for his never having been at war, for his inexperience—a complaint that Gray was making against himself at the time. She supposes a court trial of her cause against Nero's, using for his courtiers an image that is to appear in the "Ode on the Spring" and in "The Bard": "Around thee call / The gilded swarm that wantons in the sunshine / Of thy full favour. . . . "

She addresses the ghosts of those that she has caused to be murdered to raise her son to power (ll. 177–90), offering them vengeance; the evocation of the ghostly, demanding past, as has been noted, was to occur in "A Long Story," the "Elegy," "The Bard," and the "Ode for Music."

Though the fragmentary "Agrippina" is undistinguished and, as Gray was aware, fuller of sound and fury than of living passions, it has some importance in its crude statement of favorite themes and preoccupations.

"Hymn to Ignorance." Gray began and abandoned his satire on Cambridge, "Hymn to Ignorance," some time before October 1742. Its gaiety, the general tone very like that of the earlier letters from the university, and the references to Gray's rediscovery of the idiocies that he had missed for the three years of his tour, suggest that the fragment was begun before the death of West, perhaps soon after Gray's return to England. There is not much to be said for or against the "Hymn to Ignorance." It is noteworthy as Gray's first surviving experiment with the heroic couplet—a meter that, with his nagging sense of genre, must have seemed obligatory for satire. The poem is a direct echo of Pope's *Dunciad,* the fourth book of which had been published in March 1742, and which Gray had been appreciatively reading (see *C*, 1:189). It is amusing to notice in the opening four lines a burlesque intimation of the opening of the Eton College ode as well as a deliberate burlesque of Satan's greeting of Hell in *Paradise Lost, 1.* 250:

> HAIL, horrors, hail! ye ever gloomy bowers,
> Ye gothic fanes, and antiquated towres,
> Where rushy Camus' slowly-winding flood
> Perpetual draws his humid train of mud. . . .

The argument of the poem, so far as it progressed, is that the goddess Ignorance, whose seat is Cambridge, has grown lazy and sleepy and is in danger of allowing knowledge to come forth. The poet ironically praises the good old days of her reign, the Middle Ages, which were "The Schoolman's glory, and the Churchman's boast." Presumably Gray intended to survey medieval ignorance, when society was under the rule of the dismal goddess; but he stopped either because he was aware of his increasing reliance on the *Dunciad* or because of the overwhelming effect of West's death.

"The Alliance of Education and Government." A more

promising beginning is "The Alliance of Education and Government. A Fragment," Gray's only attempt at writing didactic poetry in English. W. Powell Jones argues persuasively that Gray had been carefully reading Isocrates' oration, "On the Peace," when, in 1748, he was working on this poem, and that he used the oration as a source of ideas and rhetorical techniques.[12] It is even more evident that the thesis of the "Alliance" shares ideas with Montesquieu's contemporaneous inquiry, in *De L'esprit des lois,* into the relations between character and climate (also reflected in Goldsmith's *Traveller,* Sterne's *Tristram Shandy,* and a host of essays of the time). The argument, essentially humanitarian, is that the ideal government would provide for every one the education and the opportunities with which to lead a full life.

Since the ideas have already been discussed in an earlier chapter, it remains only to be said that—apparently modeling his poem on the didactic poems of Dryden (*Religio Laici* primarily)—Gray in "The Alliance" uses the heroic couplet to aim at a thoughtful rather than a witty tone; and he writes in what for Dryden was the plain style, not so elevated as in the odes of either poet. Gray is not interested in the epigrammatic qualities of the couplet—so perfectly exploited by Pope—but in the dignity and swell of the pentameters. As a consequence, the unit of thought is not the couplet but a longer group of lines: the first thought, for completion, requires the entire twenty-one lines of the first verse paragraph.

Several passages are of interest in their reflection of other work that Gray was doing. A critical metaphor of the "Elegy," for example, appears in "The Alliance": in polar regions, Gray says,

> The Soil, tho' fertile, will not teem in vain,
> Forbids her Gems to swell, her Shades to rise,
> Nor trusts her Blossoms to the churlish Skies.

Both the hidden gem and the undeveloped flower, in the contemporaneous "Elegy" and in the future "Ode for Music," share in the dominant sorrow over possibilities unachieved and capacities undeveloped. Looking through Gray's papers as his literary executor, Mason found notes on fame (quoted in chapter 1) that seemed related to "The Alliance." If they are, they clearly tie its thesis to Gray's persistent regrets. One sentence in them most poignantly approaches not only a fundamental issue in the "Elegy" and in "The Bard" but a chief source of all art: "It is impossible to conquer that natural desire we have of being remembered; even criminal ambition and avarice, the most selfish of all passions, would wish to leave a name behind them."[13]

The survey of the high points of Western civilization, which begins eloquently in line 22 ("This spacious animated Scene survey"), again echoes a tradition much favored in Gray's period, in which Pope in "Essay on Criticism," part 3, and Thomson in "Winter" had been conspicuous practitioners and which Johnson was to join with his "Vanity of Human Wishes" and Goldsmith with *The Traveller*. As is to be expected, Gray avoids the excesses of Thomson in diction, cannot or does not wish to achieve Pope's concise wit, and in the short specimen outdoes Johnson in precision, rhythm, and elegance, though not in power or unity.

Though modern readers, having lost the taste for rhymed philosophy, are unlikely to regret that Gray abandoned "The Alliance," it has had its admirers, sometimes distinguished ones. Edmund Gosse, for example, was much impressed by the fragment, and he cites an even more luminous devotee, Edward Gibbon. However, the fragment seems mainly valuable as an interesting experiment that echoes one important image of the "Elegy" and that forecasts—in the survey and the questions about the relations between virtue and forms of government—the more emphatic, affecting, and controlled use of these themes in "The Progress of Poesy" and "The Bard."

When, toward the end of his life, Gray was asked by his young friend Nicholls why he had not completed "The Alliance," he answered that he could not undertake the labor of polishing every part of a long poem as he was accustomed to do in his shorter lyrics. Furthermore, he did not want to produce the weak parts that were necessary in a long poem to set off the strong ones (*C*, 3:1291). This is another way of saying that he found the artistic problems of the long didactic poem either insoluble or not worth solving. Although the content was important to him, his deepest convictions were against the form.

"Stanzas to Mr. Bentley." The views of literature expressed in the "Stanzas to Mr. Bentley," written in 1752 while Richard Bentley was engraving the designs for Dodsley's edition of the *Six Poems* by Gray, have been considered in chapter 2, but the poem is worth looking at in some detail because it is clearly the best of all of Gray's fragments. Actually, it is not an abandoned natural fragment, like those others considered in this section, but a completed poem that has been accidentally deformed: the manuscript that Mason found was torn at the last stanza. The verse form is that of the "Elegy," and passages, particularly lines 9–10, are strongly reminiscent of the precise diction of that poem and of its steady music and dignity. The genre—praise of a painter combined with a discussion of the relative merits of painting and poetry—is a traditional one; it had been best exemplified in English in Dryden's poem to Godfrey Kneller and in Pope's to Jervas.

In the first stanza of Gray's poem, the muse of lyric poetry is shown "Half pleas'd, half blushing." Undistinguished and quiet within the chorus of the muses, she gazes astonished as Bentley orders her sister—the muse of painting—to follow her. (The poet here is first symbolically mingled with others, but he then is selected as a model for greatness.) The transitory thoughts—the dreams, which are evanescent and beautiful, though presumably ideal and general—are given "local symmetry and life" by the painter:

> See, in their course, each transitory thought
> Fix'd by his touch a lasting essence take;
> Each dream, in fancy's airy colouring wrought,
> To local Symmetry and life awake!

The apparent compliment to the painter, however, implies that the words are far more complex, significant in far more directions, than the illustrations. In his picture (a copy in a material medium) Bentley has made solid and distinct the poetic "Fancy"; but the actual Fancy cannot be expressed by matter. It can be caught only by "airy colouring," by the shimmering quality that appears again in both of the Pindaric Odes—as the visions of Gray in "The Progress of Poesy," and as the scroll of fate that the bards unroll while they disappear. Gray's slow verses—often, as already noted, deliberately slowed in their music—now show more speed and animation; they shine with light reflected from Bentley's glowing art (an echo, perhaps, of the opening of Dryden's *Religio Laici,* in which Reason is said to be to the Soul as the borrowed light of moon and stars is to the sun). Bentley's pictures give popular appeal to Gray's lines, which till now have been "To Censure cold, and negligent of Fame": a condensed phrasing of Gray's indifference to the crowd.

With Bentley's strength, grace, inventiveness, and formal skill, Gray's poetry might overcome Pope's and Dryden's, he continues. But no one in Gray's time has "that diviner inspiration"—presumably transcending the art of Bentley—to compete with the very greatest, Shakespeare and Milton. The sixth stanza apparently amplifies the meaning of "The pomp and prodigality of Heav'n": in glorious times, when there is a towering poet, the individual inferior jewels are merged together "And dazzle with a luxury of light." The "meaner gems, that singly charm the sight," must be poets like Gray, but also like Pope and Dryden. They shine, but they do not enrich each other as they might if set around a dazzling, life-giving sun like Shakespeare or Milton. The diamond's blaze, which would add luster to their own, does not exist in this diffused age, an age without a tout ensemble. The concluding stanza, unfortunately mutilated, suggests Gray's lifelong wish to make contact with "some feeling breast" into which his lines may send a deeply felt sentiment.

"Stanzas to Bentley" is Gray's most direct and complex poetic statement of the way he sees himself in relation to other poets and to his readers. He is not so ambitious as in the contemporaneous "Progress of Poesy," which shared a dominant idea (poetry as energy source nourishing life), or so proud as in the hidden identification with the Bard; he is objective, accurate, and yet richly evocative. Through the effect of this resonant and precise diction and of the beautifully balanced images of the singing muses and the cluster of poetic jewels, Gray is authentically reasoning in poetry; he is not merely making arguments metrical.

"Ode on the Pleasure Arising from Vicissitude." Another unfinished poem by Gray, entitled by Mason "Ode on the Pleasure Arising from Vicissitude. A Fragment," seems to have been written in 1754, according to a note that Mason copied from Gray's pocket book. The note includes the rough outline for the ode: "Contrast between the Winter Past and coming Spring.—Joy owing to that Vicissitude.—Many that never feel that delight. Sloth.—Envy.—Ambition. How much happier the rustic who feels it tho' he knows not how."[14]

Certainly lighter in movement than the earlier serious poems, this ode consists of trimeter and tetrameter lines without the slower, more ponderously impressive pentameters and hexameters of the other odes; and it is also much more devoted to a straightforward delight in nature than they are. The first stanza paints a spring that could well be England's—fresh, joyous, and green—as against the literary, southern European lushness of the "Ode on the Spring." In "Ode on the Pleasure" the emphasis is on green, not purple, as the prevailing color.

The four lines in brackets Mason found nearby in Gray's commonplace book but printed at this point in his version of the fragment (*P*, 203). Together, the eight lines suggest that Gray in 1754 was anticipating Shelley's vision of the skylark, connecting the bird with both himself and his ambitious poetry:

But chief the Sky-lark warbles high
His trembling thrilling ecstasy
And, less'ning from the dazzled sight,
Melts into air and liquid light.

[Rise, my soul! on wings of fire,
Rise the rapturous choir among;
Hark! 'tis nature strikes the lyre,
And leads the general song.]

Whatever the actual connection between these quatrains, Gray surely—as in the "Stanzas to Bentley" and even more in the Pindaric Odes—asserts the exalted position of poetry. In general after the "Elegy" Gray seems confident both of the high function of his chosen profession and of his own stature within it.

The stanza following makes it even clearer than the opening that Gray is interested in that tenuous moment when winter changes to spring (a moment most useful symbolically to signify awakening, both physical and moral). Today spring is everywhere, while only yesterday there was a snowstorm. This observation calls up the reflection that only man can look forward and backward seeking joy, whereas animals in bad times merely endure in misery. The further implication, that the human present is always a tenuous balance of past and future, Gray does not explore in the fragment, though it is in his thoughts from the Eton Ode through "The Bard." In the succeeding stanza, Gray's subdued personifications help devlop the usefulness to man of reflection and hope. Like nature at the change of the seasons, Gray continues, human life is complex, combining wintry sorrows with springlike joys.

Although we cannot guess with certainty Gray's intentions, lines

41–48 (*CP* version) would seem to contain a chief thesis. They assert the kind of acceptance that gives a special dignity to Gray's best poems:

Still, where rosy Pleasure leads,
See a kindred Grief pursue;
Behind the steps that Misery treads,
Approaching Comfort view:
The hues of Bliss more brightly glow,
Chastis'd by sabler tints of woe;
And blended form, with artful strife,
The strength and harmony of Life.

This essential point of the poem is gracefully developed in the next stanza, in which the sick man recovers from his illness and delights in every manifestation of life. Presumably the concept was to be amplified in succeeding stanzas.

The fragment is promising, for its early parts show that glowing finish of expression characteristic of Gray at his best. However, the chain of routine personifications beginning about line 33 indicates that the generalized subject—because it was not an expression of anything particularly important in Gray's current world—was no longer drawing involvement from him. Like the "De Principiis Cogitandi" or "The Alliance," it deals with truisms that Gray believed but could not infuse with enough energy to sustain a poem of substantial length.

Odds and Ends. Gray's "Sketch of His Own Character. Written in 1761, and found in one of his Pocket-Books," is useful as a check on what we have been saying of his view of himself:

Too poor for a bribe, and too proud to importune,
He had not the method of making a fortune:
Could love, and could hate, so was thought somewhat odd;
No very great wit, he believed in a God.
A post or a Pension he did not desire,
But left Church and State to Charles Townshend and Squire.

As if he anticipated the persistent charge of coldness, Gray presents himself (to himself, in the privacy of his notebook) as too emotional to be a successful politician. The verses further indicate that he made the usual adjustment of the man unable or unwilling to involve himself in life: he justifies his withdrawal on the ground that life is too dirty.

In a different vein, the three fragments "The Death of Hoel," "Caradoc" and "Conan" are very effective translations from the *Gododin* of Aneurin, a Welsh bard, into heavily accented tetrameter couplets. What has been said by a student of one Welsh translation by Gray, "The Triumphs of Owen," is presumably true of the others as well: "There have been few translations of medieval Welsh poems that have so successfully captured the spirit of the original. Gray's own conciseness, elaborate artificiality in diction and syntax, and concern for the musical quality of his verse, are qualities he shares with Gwalchmai, and fit him for translating the poem.[15] They would have made most instructive samples for Gray's projected history of English literature.

Less respectable, "The Candidate," a slangy attack on the earl of Sandwich, who wanted to be high steward of Cambridge in 1764, is amusing in a rollicking way, particularly in its characterization of the various faculties of the university as elderly and repellent sisters. Sandwich is imagined as courting Physic, Law, and Divinity. Physic complains to Law that Sandwich is ugly and has a thievish look; Law answers that she has nothing against his appearance, but that his immorality is notorious. Divinity, half asleep after gorging herself on dinner and wine, hears her sisters rejecting his suit; and, in an oath-laden speech, she justifies all of his sins biblically:

> What a pother is here about wenching and roaring!
> Why David loved catches, and Solomon whoring.
> Did not Israel filch from th'Ægyptians of old
> Their jewels of silver, and jewels of gold?
> The prophet of Bethel, we read, told a lie:
> He drinks; so did Noah: he swears; so do I.
> To refuse him for such peccadillos, were odd;
> Besides, he repents, and he talks about G——.

She then offers to marry him herself, calling her sisters "a couple of Puritan bitches." This rather special poem is more in the manner one might expect from another accomplished anti-Sandwichite, Charles Churchill (who did in fact write a violent satire, also called "The Candidate," for this occasion); but Gray's attack is in its way quite successful. As might be expected, Gray did not publish it.

At the request of friends and acquaintances, Gray wrote a number of epitaphs and parts of epitaphs, a form that the twentieth century does not consider worth discussing, though Johnson devoted a considerable portion of his "Life of Pope" to that poet's proficiency in it. Gray's piece on Sir William Williams, written in 1761, is interesting for the use of the "Elegy" stanza (in which Gray had already produced his most famous epitaph, at the end of that poem); the last four lines of Mason's epitaph for his wife, for their dignity and respect; that on Mrs. Clerke, for its simplicity and generalized point; that "on a child," presumably the son of his intimate friend Dr. Thomas Wharton, for simple, universalized tenderness.

Gray's other fragments are barely worth mentioning, though the amusing ones may still give some pleasure, despite their cliquish sources and their locally allusive contents. The "Lines Spoken by the Ghost of John Dennis at the Devil Tavern," Gray's first surviving original verses in English, show a good deal of bumptious youthful fun (Gray was not quite eighteen), the pervasive influence of wide reading, and Gray's first ghostly visitor from the past. "William Shakespeare to Mrs. Anne," which Gray sent to Mason in a letter in 1765, a comic poem asking Mason's servant to prevent her master from botching Shakespeare's works, is also a purely private joke. "Satire on the Heads of Houses" (colleges at Cambridge), again a local joke, aims to hit off each of the college masters in a telling dimeter couplet. The two "Songs" done for Miss Speed, "that she might possess something from his pen on the subject of love," are standard and lifeless exercises. "Tophet," a short attack on Henry Etough, a priest overly active in local ecclesiastical politics, means nothing to posterity. The "Invitation to Mason" is an exercise in getting into eight lines as many names of their friends as Gray can. And various short impromptus have lost their point by now.

More even than his finished poems, Gray's fragments and translations show the steady experimentation in meter and subject matter that most conspicuously characterized that work. Apart from the Welsh fragments, which were designed to illustrate a stage in the development of poetry and were in one meter, and the satires, again in one meter, they indicate his concern for variation in technique. They are also, particularly in the occasional informal verse but also in such highly polished poetry as the "Stanzas to Bentley," direct reflections of Gray's personal feelings. To judge by his withdrawal of "A Long Story" after one edition and by the nakedness with which some of the unfinished pieces reveal his preoccupations, one of his criteria for polish in poetry was at least ostensible detachment on the part of the poet. These fragments and private poems thus confirm what the change in the form of the "Elegy" and in the tone from the "De Principiis" section on West to Gray's sonnet have already shown: poetry for Gray, even when confined to his notebook, was a public art, not self-expression.

The more ambitious fragments imply critical judgments by Gray that are worth glancing at. The blank verse tragedy "Agrippina" and the heroic couplet essay "The Alliance," as well as the ode to vicissitude, are in forms that Gray thought an accomplished poet ought to master. But his insufficiency as a dramatist became obvious during the process of attempting the genre. Philosophical essays in verse, aside from problems with unity, contradicted his deepest convictions about the nature of poetry. And the vicissitude poem must have seemed to him no more than a reworking of a vein that he had fully exploited earlier. Of his finished poems, only "The Progress of Poesy" may be regarded as elaborating an idea and, as I have pointed out, that very idea may well constitute its chief flaw. The "Elegy," while full of compressed wisdom, is not didactic in the sense of laying down rules for life or elaborating a system; rather, it is reflective and lyrical, like all the other original poems that Gray finished and was willing to have published with his name.

Chapter Seven

Classical or Romantic?

This study has been primarily concerned with Gray and with the nature and quality of his poems rather than with his and their place in English literature. Still, poetry is among other things a response to intellectual, particularly to literary climates in effect at a given time and place. Futhermore, if it is significant poetry, as T. S. Eliot has pointed out, it changes the way we look at what preceded it—as an outgrowth of tendencies we might not have been aware of—and by becoming a part of literary tradition it evidently affects what follows.

The most famous attempt to relate Gray to his period—by the English poet and critic Matthew Arnold—will no longer suffice, unless defining periods as unified and monolithic comes back into fashion. Arnold argued, in effect, that Gray might have been a very great poet but was thwarted by his time: "Gray, a born poet, fell upon an age of prose. He fell upon an age whose task was such as to call forth in general men's powers of understanding, wit and cleverness, rather than their deepest powers of mind and soul. . . . Poetry obeyed the bent of mind requisite for the due fulfillment of this task of the century. It was intellectual, argumentative, ingenious; not seeing things in their truth and beauty, not interpretative. Gray, with the qualities of mind and soul of a genuine poet, was isolated in his century."[1]

We wonder what this means and are perplexed how to apply it to the author of "The Bard" and the "Elegy," to say nothing of the earlier odes and the Norse translations. It is easier, perhaps, to see in it the sadness of a very similar poet, and moreover our literature's chief advocate for worshipping the very greatest art, justifying to himself his own lack of absolute greatness. The point may be valid for some artists of the eighteenth century: in a time when the poet was not expected to probe into his own most complex responses, his tendencies in that direction might be stunted so that he would waste his energy in attempting a social approach. Perhaps Oliver Goldsmith might have poured himself out more freely if he had not felt obligated to discuss agrarian economics in his most imaginative poem; certainly Johnson's "Vanity of Human Wishes" would have been different at another time, though it seems sufficiently to call forth man's deepest powers of mind and soul.

But what objective students are likely to miss in Gray is the very passion that Arnold assumes he started with, and they miss it in his life as well as his poetry. If there was a contemporary intellectual climate that affected him so strongly as Arnold says, the influence was wholly beneficial: taking Arnold's criteria, one might say that it allowed Gray to develop most fully a poetic impetus that was mild to begin with and that his tools were often "intellectual, argumentative, ingenious." If the period did indeed put a premium on bustle and material improvement, it also at least permitted the opposing ideal of retirement—preferably a fruitful retirement of doing good on an estate, as Tom Jones or Sir Charles Grandison did at precisely the time of the "Elegy," or ministering to parishioners like the vicar of Wakefield. But just being harmless, like Gray (or Sterne's Uncle Toby), was fine, particularly if, like him, you had the goad of being busy, enough sense of guilt about idleness to keep paying attention to the human condition. Indeed, in retrospect his time looks like the best ever for actually *being* the melancholy *poeta* of tradition. At least, Gray comes closest of any English poet of stature to having lived that role. From my point of view, Arnold's idea is precisely the reverse of accurate; Gray, who thought a lot about who and what he was, blamed not his times but his own limitations in the early odes, "The Progress of Poesy," and the stanzas to Bentley.

When literary historians discuss those times, they are likely to use the terms *classical* and *romantic*; and we need to see what useful meanings can be attached to these words for the purpose of placing Gray both within poetry at large and within the context of the changing temper of his time. English literature of the late seventeenth century and of the first half of the eighteenth is known to literary historians as neoclassical ("new" classical); that beginning with the publication of the *Lyrical Ballads* (1798), the joint venture of Wordsworth and Coleridge, is usually called romantic. The former is given its name because the most conspicuous writers consciously admired and imitated what they conceived to be the virtues of the Greek and Roman periods; the latter, for a variety of reasons, perhaps the most immediate of which was that some of the writers chose subjects remote in time or place from the normal concerns of Englishmen, subjects reminiscent of knightly romances. Mid-eighteenth-century critics like Johnson and novelists like Henry Fielding and Samuel Richardson used the word "romantic" to designate fanciful escapist fiction of no moral use; Coleridge, in his "Kubla Khan," gives "romantic" much more attractive connotations.

Scholars have despoiled vast forests for paper to define the differences betweeen the terms, and almost as many in hazarding definitions of the period from the middle to the end of the eighteenth century. "Pre-romantic," long in fashion, has now been abandoned on logical grounds, for, as the writers were not anticipating a new mode, they evidently did not think of themselves as "pre" anything. "Post-Augustan" (the early eighteenth century is often called the Augustan Age, after the high point of classical Roman literature) is now, with more reason, more in vogue.

What must first be agreed upon is in which of two main senses we are to use the terms *classical* and *romantic.* Shall we have them refer to distinct movements in literature, so that we may label as romantics the early nineteenth-century writers? They do seem to have some characteristics in common, dissimilar as they are in ideas, techniques, and intentions. Or shall we use the terms as referring to recurring casts of temperament, of which the movements may be special manifestations? To arrive at the orientation of Gray, it seems most useful to examine the general distinctions in orientation through their manifestation in the writers of the two contrasting periods. We shall need to enter a great many exceptions, but we shall at least have something specific to deal with.

Before we proceed to this examination, it must be understood that neither of these contrasting attitudes is ever found in its pure form in any great writer or indeed, without risk of madness, in any human being. They are always complementary as well as contrasting parts of the human mind, in the unending contrast and equilibrium produced by the search for freedom and the search for order.

The basic distinction between the terms *classical* and *romantic* as applied to temperament, it seems to me, is that between the two most clearcut views of man's underlying nature—of what Freud and his followers call the id. In the course of history, one attitude has been more emphasized at one time and the other at another: from the standpoint of English literary history, the division has been most clearly apparent in the literatures of the early eighteenth century and the early nineteenth century, presumably in some relation to the social conditions of the times. This seat of the passions and the imagination, by whatever terms it has been called, has always been recognized as the source of both creativity and mortal danger. And the chief issue separating the two temperaments is the relative emphasis on the creativity or the danger: the classical attitude tends to fear the free imagination as a sign of madness and as the parent of anarchy; but the romantic slights the risks for the sake of the riches. At no time are all the major writers dominated by the current emphasis, as witness the very classical Jane Austen slap in the middle of romanticism; and very rarely does any one great writer (like Blake) carry either view to its logical conclusion.[2] But there undoubtedly may be, as there was at each of the times specified, a general climate of attitudes collected around the aproach to man's underlying nature.

For reasons stretching back at least to the Renaissance and the Reformation, and achieving great prominence in the ferment of scientific, religious, and political changes in the seventeenth century, a complex of ideas surrounding the need for restraint, order, and limitation became dominant late in that century. Such a classical complex shows itself in literature through increasing suspicion of "fancy" and of the "passions." This fear of madness, of chaos, if the imagination is allowed complete freedom, is connected, both explicitly and implicitly, with a traditional Christian suspicion of the evils of passion and its source in original sin: the Yahoos in Swift's *Gulliver's Travels* and the dangerously lunatic narrator of his *Tale of a Tub* are the embodiment of this view. The greatest writers, being then—as ever—sensitive to the complexity of life, did not exclude one side of this basic nature of man: Swift, in the same *Gulliver's Travels,* suggests that the exclusive worship of reason (of one sort in Laputa, of another in the land of the horses) is itself a form of mad excess. Pope, in the *Essay on Man,* tries to make a synthesis of reason and passion, has a sad respect for the power of what he calls the "ruling passion," and insists that reason without passion is sterile.

In contrast to the classical insistence on restraint, romanticism emanates from a complex of ideas involving freedom of the imagination and the passions; and its most persuasive advocates form the tradition that includes Jean Jacques Rousseau, William Blake, Walt Whitman, and D. H. Lawrence. Though with many exceptions, romanticism basically assumes that man's nature is good at bottom but has been corrupted by society and thwarted in its development by sterile reason. Again, most romantics imply that this freedom is to be limited by a "natural" goodness and reason that will prevent, say, the shocking expression of the side of man's nature shown most recently in Lebanon, Northern Ireland, and South Africa.

The classical temper tends to be highly conservative and suspicious of innovations, which it regards as expressing a perverse self-importance that refuses to make the best of the world as it exists. For example, one may cite Swift's *Tale of a Tub* and, in a mass of writings tending toward the same end, his attacks on science and progress in part 3 of *Gulliver's Travels*. But one may note, as the inevitable counterpoint in the works of individual writers on different subjects, Dryden's great interest in and respect for scientific progress; Pope's reverence for Newton; and Thomson's delight in both science and the spread of commerce, a delight shared by the superclassical Addison. And Johnson, in some respects the last of the great neoclassicists, was fascinated by scientific experimentation, as was his more neoclassical contemporary Benjamin Franklin. For most of these, however, the pleasure in science lies in its utility and not in its discovery of abstract knowledge.

In literature, as we might expect, neoclassicism advocates a conservative adherence to traditional forms, styles, and subjects. One aspect of this adherence was, as critics have long noticed, imitation. Even when the imitation was comic (as in Gray's ode on the cat), the author, work, or form imitated was not thereby minimized. As W. K. Wimsatt says, we can agree "that burlesque and imitation were Augustan avenues of departure from the solemn models and constricting genre norms of the tradition, and thus of escape into a large, free realm of poetic creation . . . if only we keep reiterating the compensating principle that the escape from models *was* freedom, *was* expressive, *was* fun, only so long as the models were preserved and were present as fields of reference for the realization of the new meanings. An imitation of a classic model is always a reference *to* and only thus a departure *from* the model."[3]

Neoclassical subject matter is thus likely to be adapted to a relatively stylized use of older literary patterns: nature poetry, for example, is often based on Virgil's *Georgics* or on a pastoral tradition stretching back to the Greek poet Theocritus. Appropriate subjects are developed in meters and forms that follow ancient elegies, epics, and odes. Satires are justified by and patterned on ancient examples;

some of the most famous of the period are direct imitations—or allusions, since the author assumes the reader's familiarity with the originals and challenges comparison with them—as for example Pope's direct use of Horace and Johnson's use of Juvenal. Satire is a particularly congenial form for the cast of temper most dominant in this period, since its rational approach most clearly and instructively shows the difference between what is and what should be. As a consequence, no greater satire exists in English than the works of Dryden, Swift, Pope, Johnson, and Fielding. On the whole, there is a strong feeling about what does and does not belong in certain kinds of poetry: the view prevails that there are genres in which it is appropriate to use poetry for the expression of the different emotions or for dealing with different subjects.

The romantic attitude, by contrast, delights in innovation, since experimentation with new forms is necessary to suit new individual feelings. Blake, Wordsworth, Whitman, and Lawrence are most aware of themselves as explorers, though at times they may argue that they are merely rediscovering the past that their immediate predecessors hid. For romantics the subject matter of poetry is unlimited, and some argue that anything can legitimately be treated in any form. Of course, being practicing artists, the romantics did not carry this view to extremes—anyone who deals with words is aware that he must fuse form and content, and that he therefore must vary form with content. However, the romantic felt himself much freer to invent the form for the individual statement, or to let it evolve from the artistic conception. Coleridge, the greatest of English romantic critics, most effectively developed this conception of organic form:

> No work of true genius dares want its appropriate form, neither indeed is there any danger of this. As it must not, so genius can not, be lawless; for it is even this that constitutes its genius—the power of acting creatively under laws of its own origination. . . . The form is mechanic, when on any given material we impress a predetermined form, not necessarily arising out of the properties of the material;—as when to a mass of wet clay we give whatever shape we wish it to retain when hardened. The organic form, on the other hand, is innate; it shapes, as it develops, itself from within, and the fullness of its development is one and the same with the perfection of its outward form. Such as the life is, such is the form.[4]

In developing this theory of literary form, Coleridge was responding to the philosophical view—from one perspective the very source of nineteenth-century romanticism—that the world itself was in a state of organic becoming; it was not the static machine that previous ages had thought it.

However, romantic social applications are again diverse and unpredictable, by no means all affirming the tendencies of the French Revolution[5] that had fed the roots of romanticism. Shelley devoted himself to social and scientific experiment and innovation; Byron urged drastic social change; and Blake was an extreme revolutionary who sang democratic self-fulfillment. But Wordsworth and Coleridge, who began as social changers, ended as traditionalists; Keats, though a humanitarian and a democrat in his letters, offers no political or social doctrine in his poetry; and Carlyle and his host of followers into the present day seek the most determined sort of social regression.

The neoclassicists of the eighteenth century almost unanimously insisted that literature must be morally instructive, an attitude that had for them the corollary that it must deal with the typical, the general, from which the most can be learned by the mass of mankind. Yet Johnson, who advised poets in his *Rasselas* not to count the streaks of the tulip but to deal with the general significance of tulipness—the condensed essence of this view—wanted Boswell to fill a biography with details, no matter how minor, since there is nothing too little for so little a being as man.

The romantic attitude, as expressed by the writers of the nineteenth century, is likely to insist on the specific, the individual. This argument was also based on an ethical view, for the romantics were convinced that truth lay in details; a generalization about all mankind is true of no one man, but an exact analysis of the state of one soul will tell us things that must be true of others. William Blake, reading the *Discourses* on art of the classical Joshua Reynolds, wrote in the margin of a passage on the need for generalizing: "To Generalize is to be an Idiot. To Particularize is the Alone Distinction of Merit. General Knowledges are those Knowledges that Idiots possess."[6] In this statement, by the way, is the core of the difference in technique—localized in discussions of diction but also related to subject matter—that has caused most critics since Wordsworth to complain of the inferiority of eighteenth century poetry. This basically romantic theory is that, while prose is suitable for general statements, poetry must be specific to be true.

As a consequence of the concern for the typical and the general, the neoclassical view leads to a legalistic humanitarianism, manifested most emphatically in the American Declaration of Independence. The bases for this view go back as far as the beginning of Judaism and through Christianity, which insist that all men begin as equals before God. This tradition was reinforced in the eighteenth century by the dominance of the epistemology of John Locke, which is predicated on the equality at birth of all people who arrive with intact bodily organs and minds. It was further reinforced by a variety of ideas derived from the classics and was most effectively propagandized by the third earl of Shaftesbury as a system of harmonies in which that person is best acclimated to the universe who is best attuned to the feelings of others. In this view, the fortunate, to be in harmony with the world's order, should reach out of themselves to see that the unfortunate have souls similar to their own and suffer as much as the fortunate would in the same circumstances. Among the major works perhaps the Man in Black in Goldsmith's *Citizen of the World* and the hero of Fielding's *Tom Jones* most conspicuously embody this view of virtue. Since the necessary fellow feeling must cause men to be pained by the pain of others, the theory goes, if they have their own interests at heart they will try to cure the pain of others.

As a result, England in the eighteenth century is notable for a widespread concern for charity of all sorts (including, for example, subscriptions to aid captured enemy soldiers in the Seven Years' War with France) and for improved treatment of beggars, "fallen women," prisoners, the very poor—in general, for all those who might have been the victims of society. At the same time, some of the most conspicuous neoclassicists (such as Dryden, Pope, and Swift) insisted on political subordination on the grounds that only if everyone has his place can order be maintained—always a powerful rational response to the equally rational argument that all men are created equal.

The romantic view, again to the contrary, tends to be that every person is unique and must be sensed and judged as an individual. Such a view inevitably leads to powerful emotional assertions both for and against liberty, equality, and fraternity. Blake is intuitively certain that every human being—indeed, every bird—is a whole limitless world, and hence every person is sacred. Carlyle feels equally sure that greatness is an essence that bestows special privileges on its possessor, while no one need concern himself about inferior people.

Eigheenth-century neoclassicism often relies for its theorizing on material existence, on "reality." As Ricardo Quintana has most concisely shown, both Swift's *Tale of a Tub* and his *Gulliver's Travels* aim to prove to the average deluded person that he continually invents something different from what is before him and calls his invention the world; the consequence is that he corrupts and ruins whatever he deals with.[7] Johnson, told that one cannot refute Bishop Berkeley's argument that the world we seem to sense does not exist, kicks a stone so hard that he rebounds and says, "I refute it *thus.*" At the same time that neoclassicists assume the existence of an ideal world, usually Christian, they affirm the need to live in this one; and some, like Swift and Jane Austen, find satisfying rewards available here to the sane, decent person. To the romantic temperament—aware though it may be of the dirty socks of Swift's poem about college students—true reality exists only in exalted states, transcendental experiences, which are summed up variously in the visions of Blake; the sensuous intensities of Keats; the ecstasies of love, revolution, and damnation in Byron; Pater's insistence on burning through life with a hard, gemlike flame; Coleridge's parables about sin and redemption; or the exaltation and destruction of Moby-Dick's pursuer, Captain Ahab.

Except for this one crucial difference of transcendence, M. H. Abrams's description of the romantic lyric could apply as much to the Eton College ode as to Wordsworth's Tintern Abbey or Shelley's "Hymn to Intellectual Beauty":

> The major lyric innovation of the Romantic period . . . , the extended poems of description and meditation, are in fact fragments of reshaped autobiography, in which the poet confronts a particular scene at a significant stage of his life, in a colloquy that specifies the present, evokes the past, and anticipates the future, and thereby defines and evaluates what it means to have suffered and to grow older. In some of these poems the confrontation occurs at a time of spiritual crisis which is called "dejection" (the *acedia deiectio,* or spiritual aridity of the Christian experts of the interior life); and the ancient struggle for the blessedness of reconciliation with an alienated God becomes the attempt to recover in maturity an earlier stage

of integrity with oneself and the outer world, in a mode of consciousness for which the standard name is "joy."[8]

The difference is, of course, that Gray sees adulthood as the loss of illusions and has no hopes of this sort of joy before death, whereas Wordsworth and Shelley court states above the ordinary consciousness while in this world.

Neoclassical subject matter is likely to be social—man in relation to man—and to be concerned with practical ethics: Pope's *Essay on Man,* Johnson's *Rambler* papers, Addison and Steele's *Spectator,* Defoe's *Moll Flanders,* Richardson's *Clarissa,* Thomson's *Castle of Indolence,* Young's *Night Thoughts.* The novel, the most inevitably social of literary forms, reaches its first great peak in the eighteenth century. Such literature can be called "objective," in the sense that the writer is primarily concerned with standing off and examining the relations among men. While there may be an "I" in the novel or poem, this self is likely to be the public personality of the writer, usually revealing aspects of himself that are either neutral or creditable: Pope in his "Epistle to Dr. Arbuthnot," Gay in his *Town* Eclogues, Fielding in his novels. Though the finest works of the period, like *Gulliver's Travels,* "The Rape of the Lock," *Tom Jones,* and *Clarissa,* reveal a plentiful awareness of their authors that tendencies toward perversity exist everywhere, even in themselves, this revelation is usually by implication rather than direct statement. Romanticism, on the other hand, has frequently been called subjective. To Blake the world is how he imagines it; Wordsworth, in *The Prelude* particularly, painstakingly analyzes his own growth, omitting only what might be privately shameful; Rousseau, in his *Confessions,* tells all, perhaps even inventing shameful data. Romanticism is then often subjective in a double sense; it tends to use the author's experience overtly as material and to see the world primarily in relation to the author's sensations.

Among the interests usually said to distinguish the romantics from their predecessors was the concentration by some poets on the special qualities of peasants, of commoners generally, and by others on imagined and distant places and things. The two authors of the *Lyrical Ballads* neatly divided these subjects between themselves: Wordsworth was to treat ordinary lives so as to show their extraordinary aspects and Coleridge was to bring extraordinary events into contact with our ordinary lives. A new interest in nature is also commonly ascribed to the romantics. But while the increased emphases are beyond question, the reader should be cautious in assuming that there was a sharp cleavage in subject matter. Swift, Gay, and Thomson, in the heart of neoclassicism, dealt perhaps too exactly with the lives of ordinary men in poetry, and the novelists did so in prose, as did the playwrights. The eighteenth century also provides a good many examples of attempts to exploit the exotic: in the Celtic revival lurking through the century and appearing prominently from "The Bard" onward; in the cult of the Chinese and Oriental in general that derived from the mercantile contact with the East and from the translation of the *Arabian Nights;* and in the aesthetic of the sublime. The "Oriental Tale," for example, became a recognized genre, or rather a whole group of recognized genres. And there are quite a few fine nature poems, beginning with Denham's famous "Cooper's Hill" in the late seventeenth century and featuring Pope's "Windsor Forest" and his eclogues—to say nothing of the *Seasons* of Thomson (written in the 1720s, the height of the neoclassical period, though often cited as "preromantic" in its minute examination of nature). If we recognize that the old generalizations are based on the best surviving works only, and if we think of the great mass of rightly forgotten novels and magazine stories and verses, we will have even less confidence in the simple distinctions.

Finally, neoclassical writing, as a consequence of its insistence on the general and the morally useful, is likely to be more discursive than that of the romantics and to use elaborate personifications rather than consciously developed and structurally dominant symbols. Again, this distinction cannot be absolute, since all art involves significance; and significance inevitably entails symbolism. In his "Modest Proposal," for example, Swift symbolizes the inhuman exploitation of the Irish in a plan for their rulers to eat Irish babies; in Pope's "Rape of the Lock," the lock itself becomes the symbol of a way of life. Such basically symbolic undercurrents as the subject—the childhood idyll as against adult evil—of the "Deserted Village," or such conscious symbols as the pyramids of *Rasselas* or the girdle in William Collins's "Ode on the Poetical Character" are other examples.

The romantics, on the whole, have a stronger—and poetically more appealing—tendency to represent a perception in a fresh symbol rather than to personify or discuss it, to avoid what T. S. Eliot called the prose linkages, and to concentrate on the poetic stuff of metaphor. They tend to a greater exploitation of both the conscious and unconscious symbols that reach into the hman psyche and expand there, as in Blake's tiger or Shelley's west wind or the Wuthering Heights farm. Coleridge's "Kubla Khan," for example, is a poem about the creative power of the imagination; but instead of using the word "imagination," he pictures its action as follows:

A damsel with a dulcimer
In a vision once I saw:
It was an Abyssinian maid,
And on her dulcimer she played,
Singing of Mount Abora.
Could I revive within me
Her symphony and song,
To such a deep delight 'twould win me,
That with music loud and long,
I would build that dome in air,
That sunny dome! those caves of ice!

Goldsmith, in "The Deserted Village," also conceives of the poetic imagination as a girl. But he is far more explicit and therefore, despite the tenderness and clarity of the diction, far more limited in the response that he evokes:

And thou, sweet Poetry, thou loveliest maid,
Still first to fly where sensual joys invade;
Unfit in these degenerate times of shame,
To catch the heart, or strike for honest fame;
Dear, charming nymph, neglected and decried,
My shame in crowds, my solitary pride.
Thou source of all my bliss, and all my woe,
That found'st me poor at first, and keep'st me so;
Thou guide by which the nobler arts excel,
Thou nurse of every virtue, fare thee well.

On the basis of these various criteria, we may try to see where Gray belongs by temperament and historical classification. Like everyone, he had tendencies in both directions; and, like the Victorian Matthew Arnold, he lived in a time that lay socially and intellectually between two worlds, one dying, the other struggling to be born. H. J. C. Grierson sees him as a master of the past looking uncertainly ahead: "Gray's taste was not satisfied with the poetry of his own day . . . his poetic instinct led him to cast both behind and before, while yet he had not the strength of inspiration or courage of temperament to be a rebel in more than a very tentative fashion; and so Gray's poetry is at once the perfect flower of our Augustan age and carries within it the seeds of the romantic revival." To such connection with tradition Bertrand Bronson adds that Gray loved "tradition*s*": "In whatever direction [Pindaric, Miltonic, Scandinavian, Celtic], he probed for the quintessential, delighting to *report*—to bring home—the special virtues of each kind."[9]

In respect to the first and basic division between complexes of ideas, for example, Gray seems to live in the best of both worlds. He is wedded to the ideas of order and regularity, as is evidenced by his extraordinary care as a craftsman, his elaborate and successful reliance on the most confining meters and metrical devices. At the same time he constantly strives, particularly in the two Pindaric Odes, to stretch the substance and appeal of his work beyond reason: he insists that the highest poetry, lyric poetry, demands a kind of demonic possession of the poet that communicates its transports to the reader, and he steadily exalts "fancy" or imagination at the expense of bare reason. He sees as a real misfortune his lack of the basic gusto—the deep involvement in human life—of those writers, like Shakespeare and Milton, whom he most admires. He yearns for the intensity and freedom with which to pour himself completely into living.

But this misfortune, which is also the underlying subject of much that he wrote, has its advantages. Better than anyone else, he was able to make use of his era's reliance on order in stretching his relatively thin and sporadic inspiration to its utmost. In the earlier works, through the "Elegy," his achievement lay in infusing life into a number of traditional forms through an exquisite delicacy of ear, superb metrical craftsmanship, command over diction and picture, and an ability to feel in each conception something with a shape adaptable to his own deepest predilections. Each of his completed and published poems is in a form at least slightly different from every other one, for he persists in experimentation. In every attempt, he uses a form sanctioned by tradition (though his Scandinavian and Celtic experiments follow a tradition foreign and shocking to some of his neoclassical readers); he sees what it can yield him and then he tries another innovation.

Gray's genius is not in inventing the completely new (though one wonders which of the great poets, aside from Blake in his artistically monstrous prophetic books, invented where there was nothing in the past to work with). Rather, Gray brings some traditions to a perfection of concentration and purity, as in the Eton College ode and in the "Elegy." To other traditions, as in the Pindaric Odes, he restores a wholeness of life of which earlier imitators had lost sight. By fusing wilder strains from the Gothic into the orderly Greek patterns, he brings a sense of the complementary elements of life to forms that had become petrified in mere rhetorical exercises. He is, therefore, at the summit of a development from the past in "The Bard," not an innovator in form or subject. But, by his inclusion of material that had not previously been seen as appropriate to this development, he opened paths for further exploration.

On the question of the distinction between the general and the particular, Gray is solidly classical in theory and practice. He is purely classical in his belief that art should be concerned with what Plato called the ideal world of being and not with the material and shifting world of becoming. All of his work—including the change in the ending of the "Elegy"—aims to remove himself as a special case from the poem and to substitute a generalized personality, partaking of idealized qualities of his own, who can speak of one side of mankind. This intention is most apparent in the difference between his Latin passage on the death of West in his "De Principiis Cogitandi" and his English sonnet on the same subject, but it also appears in everything else that he wrote, notably in the "Elegy" and in the Pindaric Odes. In "The Progress of Poesy," for example, Shakespeare, Milton, Dryden, and Gray are themselves and, more importantly, also types of imaginative poets. Anything that seems idiosyncratic is made a symptom of the general: Milton's blindness is not a personal misfortune but an illustration of the brilliance with which the light of truth and beauty, of God, strikes a mortal observer's eye. In "The Bard" the historical events prophesied are to be seen as the variegated horrors that attend the consequences of tyranny, not as the specific destinies of Edward I's posterity; and the symbolic suicide at the end is the disdain of the bard for the materialistic tyrant.

Gray's language, as has been pointed out, is designed to achieve the maximum of generalization combined with a maximum of musical and spectacular evocation—an aim that leads to a compression and novelty objectionable to the neoclassical side of Johnson and at the same time to an apparently perverse calculation of the sort the romantic Wordsworth disliked. The diction changes, as Gosse and others have observed, from the relatively standardized though precise and haunting personifications of Gray's youth—best shown in the Eton College ode and in the "Elegy"—to the more specific, fresh, and realistic phrasing of the Scandinavian translations. The Pindaric Odes, at a stage in between, offer the splendor of the earlier work with a minimum of its abstractness. In this respect, as in others, one can see a turning point in Gray's career separating the "Elegy," which can fairly be called the highest expression of Gray as the traditionalist working only with elements sanctioned by the past, from the Pindaric Odes, in which he introduces added substance to the tradition.

Gray uses the ideal for moral reasons, or at least can justify it that way on the ground that it makes little useful difference to the world whether one young man is unsure how to spend his life (as for example in the "Ode on the Spring") while the state of unsure, sensitive youthfulness is very much worth portraying. However, he is far less interested in the moral uses of poetry than are the theorists of his time. He once wrote to West that the phrase "didactic poetry" might well be a logical contradiction; and, though his writings are full of reflections on man's nature, they do not have didactic aims. The "Ode on the Spring" does not pretend to teach how man is to spend his life; rather it presents the dilemma of youth faced by life's apparent meaninglessness. The Eton ode offers no solution but that of the "Ode to Adversity"—sympathy for others—again with the emphasis on picturing the state rather than on solving its problem with a moral imperative. The "Elegy" lays down no rules for facing death but instead reveals the narrator's response to models of living and dying; and it ends with an epitaph to one who was overcome by contemplating the theme.

Paradoxically, the more "romantic" Pindaric Odes seem to offer didactic statements. The first has been condemned by the very advocates of didacticism; the second has been far more successful precisely because it presents the argument dramatically and spectacularly instead of asserting it directly. When we compare "The Bard" with Johnson's "Vanity of Human Wishes"—surely the best traditionally neoclassical poem since Pope—we note Johnson's vigorous insistence on the title theme at every point and on his detailed (though obscure) program at the end for achieving peace. Gray's concern is always for the picture, the visual symbol—a characteristic concern of his time,[10] but also one that romantics were to exploit. He is likely, however, particularly in the earlier poems, to reflect discursively in the older manner; or perhaps he can be said to conceive of poetry (before "The Bard") as a representation of states of the soul through a mixture of image and thought.

Politically and socially, Gray shares the humanitarianism of his day, but it is complicated for him by two conflicting tendencies. On the one hand, his fastidiousness makes him feel set off from the world: he is either above it, as he says at times; or he is below it, as Roger Martin persuasively argues. More likely this fastidiousness is a result of an ambiguous compound of the two: he condemns the self that he cherishes for fearfulness and praises it for sensitivity. On the other hand, he is subject to a yearning for fellow feeling that he manages to infuse into his best earlier work, notably the Eton ode and the "Elegy." If, as has recently been argued, mid-eighteenth-century literature showed a special sense of equality in the generalized, observing self's view of the idiosyncratic acting self—Johnson's sympathy with man's plight in *Rasselas,* or Sterne's in *Tristram Shandy,* as against Swift's contempt for that side of the self that his satirized spokesmen represent—then those mid-century poems perfectly suit their time.[11] The Pindaric Odes again exhibit a kind of romantic apartness of the Bard as leader and savior that anticipates Burns, Wordsworth, Coleridge, and Shelley. In these later poems also, as well as in his translations, Gray shares the romantic view (derived at least partly from the idea of the sublime, which is comprised in the neoclassical aesthetic), that the reality suitable for poetry exists in the highest transports of the imagination. Characteristically, Gray finds his justification in a poet of the past, Pindar, whom he strives in vain to emulate in this respect.

As has been suggested, Gray is fully settled in the poetic traditions; in fact, he outdoes his contemporaries in his concern for maintaining the proper genres. Along with the odes of William

Collins, Gray's are the only important "regular" Pindarics, repudiations of the laxer form popular before him. His satires and fragment of a didactic poem are in the obligatory heroic couplet; his fragment of a tragedy, in dutiful blank verse; his shorter odes, in forms clearly reminiscent of Horace and other ancient models; and his "Elegy," in the stanza agreed on as appropriate for melancholy reflections and in a meter sanctioned by the practice of Tibullus. At the same time that genres seem only reasonable to him (as to a certain extent they have been so even to most romantic poets—Shelley's elegy on Keats is not written in the ballad stanza, nor is Wordsworth's *Prelude*), Gray objects to rigidity in adherence to them, or indeed to any rules of criticism. While Gray does not go so far afield as the great romantics in seeking variations in verse forms, his incorporation of Scandinavian and Welsh rhythms into the English tradition is as experimental as Byron's borrowing of Italian forms or as Keats's fusion of sonnet patterns for his odes.

Gray's subject matter is largely limited in the earlier poems to literary sources, and the scenery often comes from the classics rather than from his countryside. Even in "The Bard" the pictures are influenced by Italian Renaissance painting. At least in those works written and completed for the few whom he considered competent judges, he relies heavily on topics deriving from traditional practice. His imagination is tied to elevated, distinctively "poetic" pictures; though in the "Elegy" he achieves a distillation of ordinary life with sure touches, most of them have literary antecedents. He is not enough interested in other people generally to care about the details of their lives, as Wordsworth cares self-consciously and Byron naturally.

But Gray is fascinated by other modes of living, the more exotic the better. As W. Powell Jones showed, Gray's reading interests were about evenly divided between history and travel books. When he finds a mode that means something in his search for a way out of the bounds of reason and gentility, a way to perceive and express the powerful and irrational urges that he shares with mankind, he seizes on it and incorporates it, no matter how violent: hence the gory primitive chants and tales that he translated so effectively. The test of poetic subject matter for Gray is always its degree of relevance to the pictures and music with which he wants to communicate the ideal.

Finally, though Gray does not overtly explore himself for poetic material, in the way Wordsworth, Rousseau, or Whitman can, and though he insists that a screen between his unique self and the reader is necessary both for propriety and for the essential poetic idealization, in his work a recognizable human voice calls out to its brothers. If this decorous objectivity is the sign of the classicist—and I am not at all sure that it is—then Gray combines with it an insistent assertion of his underlying emotional state. Such an assertion, in its combination of diffidence and pride, fear of life and bravery in seeking beyond the limits of the known, concern for the self stretching out to concern for the identical aspects of mankind, would seem, as a necessary complement, romantic.

Rather than say, with Arnold, that Gray was a born poet doomed to prose by a prosaic age, we should consider him the perfect spokesman for a poetic age that is unclear in its position on the great and recurrent human problems—and notably on those dealing with the relations between the rational and the nonrational. Aware of this deficiency both in his time and in himself, Gray is better able than any one of his English contemporaries to work from a firm basis in the rational into an exploration of the irrational. From a peak of the classical, he opens vistas for romanticism.

Such a position inevitably entails an effect on his successors. Apart from his contemporary vogue, which filled magazines in the British Isles and America with elegies and Pindaric odes, his lasting influence on English literature and on our cultural heritage as readers of English has been pervasive. He inaugurated the Celtic revival, which in turn strongly reinforced the bardic ideal—the ideal of the poet as prophet and patriot—that is so important to Shelley, Byron, Keats, Tennyson, Whitman, and Yeats. His is an eloquent voice speaking for the freeing of the imagination; though the romantics after Blake (and Blake loved him) decried his diction, they paid him the compliment, sometimes unconscious, of imitation. Wordsworth professedly wrote his "Ode to Duty" in the form of Gray's "Ode to Adversity." Shelley's "To a Skylark" echoes Gray's unfinished (but posthumously printed and available from 1775) ode to vicissitude in its central image. We catch other indications of influence in casual lines and passages. Shelley's Prometheus is told, in a line borrowed from "The Bard," that "Past ages crowd on thee" (*Prometheus Unbound,* 1:561); Byron's famous description of the gaiety in Brussels on the eve of Waterloo seems to expand the passage on Richard II's reign in "The Bard"; Hardy entitles a book *Far From the Madding Crowd,* assuming everyone will recognize the passage in the "Elegy"; in *Purple Dust* Sean O'Casey names a couple of tradition-bound Englishmen Stoke and Poges, with a similar assumption about the setting of that poem.[12] But citing specific examples of influence means little with a poet like Gray; his poetry has become part of all of us, readers and writers alike.

Gray's achievement was great, despite his obvious deficiencies—the lack of deeply passional involvement, of the emotional variety and intensity characteristic of the greatest masters. As compensation, he offers the most responsible sense of craftsmanship in English poetry—a sense that requires of him both perfection of finish and persistent experimentation. Though he wrote relatively little, that little included some of the most finished classical odes in the language; one of the finest reflective poems that we have, and surely the most beloved; Pindaric Odes of a unique splendor; and the first exploration, in beautifully polished work, of a rich vein of poetry that has yielded treasures to others as well. Finally, whatever criteria or terms we will apply to Gray's achievements, or however we place him in his time or another, we know that in the most important respect he accomplished the rarest of artistic feats: the creation of one work at least that is not for critics or antiquarians alone, but for all readers.

Notes and References

Preface

1. *Critical Review* 28 (1775):460–61.

Chapter One

1. R. W. Ketton-Cremer, *Thomas Gray* (Cambridge: Cambridge University Press, 1955), 61, 64, 100, 101–2.

2. Roger Martin, *Essai sur Thomas Gray* (London: Oxford University Press, 1935), 4.

3. Ibid., 9. See also app. A, "The Case Submitted to Dr. Audley," in *Correspondence,* ed. Paget Toynbee and Leonard Whibley (Oxford: Clarendon Press, 1971), 3:1195–97, for Mrs. Gray's charges against Philip Gray. *Correspondence* hereafter cited in the text as *C.*

4. Martin, *Essai,* 14, 20.

5. Quoted in C. G. Osgood, "Lady Phillipina Knight and Her Boswell," *Princeton University Library Chronicle* 4 (1943):48.

6. Quoted by Leonard Whibley in his preface to *Ode on the Pleasure arising from Vicissitude* (San Francisco: Wm. Andrews Clark Library, 1933), viii. On the fastidiousness, W. Powell Jones has found new information: "In dress he was meticulous: the various portraits attest it, but the best evidence is from the expense accounts of his trips to London, where the most prominent items, including his indulgences in snuff and the theater, are for personal adornment." See Jones, "Mute Inglorious Gray," *Emory University Quarterly* 11 (1955):205. One reviewer of Mason's *Memoirs* of Gray, John Langhorne, who might have met Gray or gossiped about him in a brief residence at Cambridge around 1760, sneers at Gray's earlier rumored effeminate manner, *Monthly Review* 53 (1775):101–2.

7. See *Correspondence,* 1:303, n. 2; 2:653, n. 2; 3:998.

8. See ibid., 3:1216–20 (app. J, "Gray's Removal from Peterhouse to Pembroke").

9. Leslie Stephen, "Gray and His School," *Cornhill Magazine* 40 (1879):74.

10. William Temple, "A Sketch of the Character of the Celebrated Mr. Gray, Author of the Elegy in a Country Church-yard," *London Magazine* 41 (1772):140.

11. Samuel Johnson, *Lives of the English Poets,* ed. G. B. Hill (Oxford: Clarendon Press, 1905), 3:421.

12. James Boswell, *Life of Johnson,* ed. G. B. Hill, rev. L. F. Powell (Oxford: Clarendon Press, 1934), 2:327.

13. William Mason, in prefatory *Memoirs of His Life and Writing,* bound with Mason's edition of *Poems of Mr. Gray* (York: A. Ward, 1775), 403.

14. Ibid., 145.

15. Jean Hagstrum sympathetically discusses Gray's emotional attachments in "Gray's Sensibility," in *Fearful Joy: Papers from the Thomas Gray Bicentenary Conference at Carleton University,* ed. James Downey and Ben Jones (Montreal: McGill-Queen's University Press, 1974), 6–19.

16. Mason, *Memoirs,* 202–3.

17. See "The Motives for Writing: A Dream," *Court Magazine* 1 (1761):167–69, and M. Golden, "A Decade's Bent: Names in the *Monthly Review* and the *Critical Review,* 1760–1769," *Bulletin of the New York Public Library* 79 (1976):352–53.

18. The most useful discussion of the depth and range of Gray's studies is W. Powell Jones's *Thomas Gray, Scholar* (Cambridge, Mass.: Harvard University Press, 1937).

19. For a discussion of this pattern, see M. Golden, "The Imagining Self in the Eighteenth Century," *Eighteenth Century Studies* 3 (1969):4–27.

Chapter Two

1. His most extended discussion of deism and his attack on Shaftesbury's philosophy occur in a letter of 18 August 1758, to his friend Richard Stonhewer (*Correspondence,* 2:582–83); the warning is in Nicholls' "Reminiscences of Gray," in ibid., 3:1289.

2. See Jones, *Thomas Gray* 21 and "The Vogue of Natural History in England, 1750–1770," *Annals of Science* 2: (1937): 345–52; H. T. Swedenberg, Jr., "Thomas Gray's 'Journal for 1754 from the First of March,' " *Huntington Library Quarterly* 3 (1939):77–102.

3. W. K. Wimsatt, "Imitation as Freedom—1717–1798," *New Literary History* 1(1970):217.

4. Walter J. Bate, *From Classic to Romantic* (Cambridge, Mass.: Harvard University Press, 1946), 46–47.

5. Still the best discussion of the nature and history of the idea of the sublime in eighteenth-century aesthtics is Samuel H. Monk, *The Sublime: A Study of Critical Theories in XVIII-Century England* (New York: Modern Language Association, 1935).

6. Samuel Kliger, *The Goths in England* (Cambridge, Mass.: Harvard University Press, 1952), 3.

7. Bertrand H. Bronson, "The Pre-Romantic or Post-Augustan Mode," *ELH: A Journal of English Literary History* 20 (1953): 22.

8. This double attitude appears in Gray's journal entry about the same time. See Edmund Gosse, ed., *The Works of Thomas Gray* (New York: A. C. Armstrong, 1885), 1:244.

9. "Gray's Notes of Travel," in Duncan C. Tovey, *Gray and His Friends* (Cambridge: Cambridge University Press, 1890), 220.

10. Mason, ed., *Poems of Mr. Gray,* 87.

11. See Herbert W. Starr, Gray as a Literary Critic (Philadelphia: University of Pennsylvania Press, 1941), passim, esp. 104–5.

12. *Monthly Review* 38 (1768):408. For authorship of this anonymous review and the one cited in Chap. 1, n.6 above, see Benjamin Christie Nangle, *The Monthly Review. First Series 1749-1789.* Indexes of *Contributors* (Oxford:Clarendon Press, 1934), 116, 236.

13. Mason, *Memoirs,* 233–34.

14. *Works,* ed. Gosse, 1:331–32.

15. For the significance of personifications in Gray's time, see Earl R. Wasserman, "The Inherent Values of 18th Century Personifications," *Publications of the Modern Language Association* 65 (1950):435–63; Morton W. Bloomfield, "A Grammatical Approach to Personification Allegory," *Modern Philology* 60 (1963):161–71; Margaret Anne Doody, *The Daring Muse: Augustan Poetry Reconsidered* (Cambridge: Cambridge University Press, 1985), 163–71.

Chapter Three

1. See *The Complete Poems,* ed H. W. Starr and J. R. Hendrickson (Oxford: Clarendon Press, 1966), 152; hereafter my text for Gray's poems, cited as *CP*.

2. Ketton-Cremer, *Thomas Gray,* 61.

3. George N. Shuster, *The English Ode from Milton to Keats* (New York: Columbia University Press, 1940), 10.

4. Mason, ed., *Poems of Mr. Gray,* 75.

5. Johnson, *Lives of the English Poets,* 3:434.

6. Martin, *Essai*, 393.

7. For this poem, and for all others, the fullest survey of sources is in *The Poems of Thomas Gray, William Collins, Oliver Goldsmith,* ed. Roger Lonsdale (London: Longmans Green, 1969); hereafter cited in the text as *P*.

8. Oliver Elton, *A Survey of English Literature, 1730–1780* (London: Edward Arnold, 1928), 2:58–59.

9. Preface to *Lyrical Ballads* (2d ed.), in *Poetical Works,* ed. E. de Selincourt (Oxford: Clarendon Press, 1944), 1:391.

10. Jones, *Thomas Gray, Scholar,* 8.

11. See Patrcia Meyer Spacks, "Statement and Artifice in Thomas Gray," *Studies in English Literature* 5 (1965):524; Judith K. Moore, "Thomas Gray's 'Sonnet on the Death of Richard West': The Circumstances and the Diction," *Tennessee Studies in Literature* 19 (1974):113. Lonsdale (*Poems,* 65), covers the great range of allusions, noting particularly a whole sonnet

of Petrarch's that uses very similar images to express the rejected lover's alienation; Ernest Dilworth, "Landor on Gray's Sonnet on the Death of West," *Notes & Queries* 15 (1968):215, quotes another very similar poem on unreunited love by the French sixteenth-century poet Jean Antoine de Baif.

12. *The Correspondence of Gerard Manley Hopkins and Richard Watson Dixon,* ed. Claude Colleer Abbott (London: Oxford University Press, 1955), 137. For a good discussion of Wordsworth's motives, see James E. Swearingen, "Wordsworth on Gray," *SEL* 14 (1974):489–509.

13. Norman Maclean, "From Action to Image: Theories of the Lyric in the Eighteenth Century," in *Critics and Criticism,* ed. R. S. Crane (Chicago: University of Chicago Press, 1952), 437.

14. Johnson, *Lives of the English Poets,* 3:435–36.

15. Frontispiece for "Hymn [sic] to Adversity" in *Designs by Mr. Bentley for Six Poems by Mr. T. Gray* (London: R. Dodsley, 1753).

16. Samuel Taylor Coleridge, *Biographia Literaria,* ed. J. Shawcross (London: Oxford University Press, 1954), 1:12.

17. Johnson, *Lives of the English Poets.* 3:434–35.

18. Elton, *Survey,* 2:62. For useful discussions of the Eton College ode, see also Albert M. Lyles, "Historical Perspective on Gray's Eton College Ode," *Tennessee Studies in Literature* 9 (1964):57–61; Frank H. Ellis, "Gray's Eton College Ode: the Problem of Tone," *Papers on Language and Literature* 5 (1969);130–38; Thomas B. Gilmore, Jr., "Allusion and Melancholy in Gray's *Ode on a Distant Prospect of Eton College,*" *PLL* 15 (1979):52–58; Robert Micklus, "Voices in the Wind: The Eton Ode's Ambivalent Prospect of Maturity," *English Language Notes* 18 (1981):181–86; and particularly Margaret Anne Doody, *The Daring Muse* (Cambridge: Cambridge University Press, 1985), who reproduces Bentley's design and brilliantly comments on it (165).

19. Gosse, in his *Gray* (119), makes this point very clearly: "His poems, whatever they are, are never chains of consecutive stanzas; each line, each group of lines, has its proper place in a structure that could not be shorter or longer without a radical re-arrangement of ideas." Martin impressively analyzes the techniques by which Gray's stanzas are made integral "cells" of his unified odes, in the *Essai,* 403–6.

20. *Critical Review* 25 (1768):367.

21. Johnson, *Lives of the English Poets,* 3:434.

22. David Cecil, "The Poetry of Thomas Gray," in *Eighteenth Century English Literature,* ed. James L. Clifford (New York: Oxford University Press, 1959), 249; Martin, *Essai,* 376; Robert Pattison, "Gray's 'Ode on the Death of a Favourite Cat': A Rationalist's Aesthetic," *Univeristy of Toronto Quarterly* 49 (1979–80):160.

23. Elton, *Survey,* 2:62.

Chapter Four

1. Mason, *Memoirs,* 157.
2. These are the essential conclusions of *Correspondence,* app. I, "The Composition of the Elegy" (3:1214–16), and of Lonsdale, who exhaustively surveys the evidence and conjectures (*Poems,* 103–10).
3. Mason, ed., *Poems of Mr. Gray,* 108.
4. Johnson, *Lives of the English Poets,* 3:441–42.
5. Amy Louise Reed, *The Background of Gray's Elegy* (New York: Columbia University Press, 1924), 125–26.
6. William Shenstone, *Works* (London: R. & J. Dodsley, 1764), 1:4–7.
7. After some decades of inconclusive discussion of which of the two, Shenstone or Gray, influenced the other in the writing of elegy, Herbert W. Starr, in his excellent survey of the background and publication of the "Elegy," in *Twentieth Century Interpretations of Gray's Elegy* (Englewood Cliffs, N.J.: Prentice-Hall, 1968), 6, concludes that "the resemblances were probably coincidental."
8. Margery Bailey, "Edward Young," in *The Age of Johnson: Essays Presented to Chauncey Brewster Tinker* (New Haven: Yale University Press, 1949), 205.
9. For a discussion of the sources and effects of Hammond's work, see J. Fisher, "James Hammond and the Quatrain of Gray's *Elegy,*" *Modern Philology* 32 (1932):301–10.
10. Elton, *Survey,* 2:67. Michael Wilding, "The Epitaph to Gray's Elegy: Two Early Printings and a Parody," *Notes & Queries* (1968) 15:213–214, has found the third stanza of the "Epitaph" "included in a nineteenth century 'repertory of inscriptions suitable for tombs and monuments' " (213).
11. *British Magazine* 6 (February 1751):101.
12. William Empson, *Some Versions of Pastoral* (London: Chatto & Windus, 1935), 4. Howard D. Weinbrot, "Gray's *Elegy:* A Poem of Moral Choice and Resolution," *Studies in English Literature* 18 (1978):537–51, seems to support Empson's view at least with respect to the subject of the "Epitaph," who shows "unselfish acceptance" of God's disposal of him (548); Roger Elliott, "The Bard as Moping Owl," *Cambridge Quarterly* 15 (1986):207–15, sees the language of the "Elegy" as refuting Empson's charge.
13. Over a century ago, W. Elwin, reviewing Mitford's edition of Gray in the *Quarterly Review* 94 (December 1853):47, complained that the "transition from the general reflection to himself was an unhappy afterthought. . . . " F. W. Bateson, speaking *ex cathedra* in his *English Poetry: A Critical Introduction* (London: Longmans, Green, 1950) says that "The first critical point that must be made in any discussion of the poem is the

inferiority of the last fifty-six lines" (183), while "the sixteen cancelled lines, which rounded off the original poem," "are superb" (185). More temperately, George Sherburn speaks of Gray's "discarding four noble quatrains" while admiring the thematic value of Gray's change. See his edition of *An Elegy Wrote in a Country Church Yard* and *The Eton College Manuscript,* Augustan Reprint Society, no. 31 (Los Angeles, 1951); iv–v.

14. Cleanth Brooks, *The Well Wrought Urn: Studies in the Structure of Poetry* (New York: Reynal & Hitchcock, 1947), 99–100.

15. Ibid., 105–6.

16. Ibid., 107.

17. Ibid., 109–10.

18. Frank H. Ellis, "Gray's *Elegy:* The Biographical Problem in Literary Criticism," *Publications of the Modern Language Association* 65 (1951):981, 983. Brooks's and Ellis's essays have been reprinted in Starr's *Twentieth Century Interpretations.*

19. Odell Shepard, "A Youth to Fortune and to Fame Unknown," *Modern Philology* 20 (1923):347–73; the clearest refutation, H. W. Starr, " 'A Youth to Fortune and to Fame Unknown: A Re-Estimation," *Journal of English and Germanic Philology* 48 (1949):97–107.

20. Ellis, "Gray's *Elegy,*" 987.

21. Ibid., 999.

22. Ibid., 1003.

23. Among the early ones are: Morse Peckham, "Gray's 'Epitaph' Revisited," *Modern Language Notes* 71 (1956):409–11; John H. Sutherland, "The Stonecutter in Gray's 'Elegy,' " *Modern Philology* 55 (1957):11–13; and A. E. Dyson, "The Ambivalence of Gray's Elegy," *Essays in Criticism* 7 (1957):257–61. Apart from those pieces so far noted, and other fine ones in *Twentieth Century Interpretations,* ed. Starr, and in *Fearful Joy,* ed. Downey and Jones, a pair of able essays shows Gray's effective exploitation of verbal ambiguity: George Watson, "The Voice of Gray," *Critical Quarterly* 19, no. 4 (1977): 51–57 and W. Hutchings, "Syntax of Death: Instability in Gray's *Elegy Written in a Country Churchyard,*" *Studies in Philology* 81 (1984):496–514.

24. Irene Tayler, "Two Eighteenth-Century Illustrators of Gray," in *Fearful Joy,* ed. Downey and Jones, 122; Doody, *The Daring Muse,* 192.

25. Lawrence Lipking, "Quick Poetic Eyes: Another Look at Literary Pictorialism," in *Articulate Images: The Sister Arts from Hogarth to Tennyson,* ed. Richard Wendorf (Minneapolis: University of Minnesota Press, 1983), 18.

Chapter Five

1. Jones, *Thomas Gray, Scholar.* 15.

2. William Congreve, "A Discourse on the Pindaric Ode," in *The Works of the English Poets,* ed. Alexander Chalmers (London, 1810), 10:300.

3. Ibid.

4. W. Powell Jones, "The Contemporary Reception of Gray's *Odes,*" *Modern Philology* 28 (1930):61–82.

5. *Literary Magazine* 2 (1757):426.

6. Ibid, 468.

7. Oliver Goldsmith, *Collected Works,* ed. Arthur Friedman (Oxford: Clarendon Press, 1966), 1:113–14.

8. Ibid., 114.

9. Jean Hagstrum, *The Sister Arts* (Chicago: University of Chicago Press, 1958), 304.

10. Johnson, *Lives of the English Poets,* 3:436.

11. John Mitford, ed., *Works of Thomas Gray* (London: Wm. Pickering, 1835), 1:xviii.

12. Lonsdale (*Poems,* 160) valuably discusses this genre of "progress poem" in Gray's day.

13. Johnson, *Lives of the English Poets,* 3:437.

14. See James Steele, "Thomas Gray and the Season for Triumph," in *Fearful Joy,* ed. Downey and Jones, 198–240, and Howard D. Weinbrot, "Gray's 'Progress of Poesy' and 'The Bard': An Essay in Literary Transmission," in *Johnson and His Age,* ed. James Engell (Cambridge, Mass.: Harvard University Press, 1984), 311–32.

15. Jones, *Thomas Gray, Scholar,* 96.

16. "Cambri," in *Chronologie de la vie et de l'oeuvre de Thomas Gray,* by Roger Martin (Paris: Presses Universitaires de France, 1931), 176.

17. Johnson, *Lives of the English Poets,* 3:439.

18. Hagstrum, *The Sister Arts,* 313. In a tribute to Gray's formal achievement in "The Bard," Irvin Ehrenpreis adds to the scenic significance of the conclusion: "Finally, in a gesture that reverses his opening challenge when he looked down from a beetling rock upon the descending army of invaders, the bard leaps trimphantly to his suicide in the 'roaring tide' of the river" (*Literary Meaning and Augustan Values* [Charlottesville: University of Virginia Press, 1974], 89).

19. Ibid., 314.

20. Johnson, *Lives of the English Poets,* 3:440.

21. Jones, *Thomas Gray, Scholar,* 15. Arthur Johnston, "Gray's Use of the Gorchest Y Beirdd in 'The Bard', " *Modern Language Review* 59 (1964):335–38, points out the difference between Gray's use of the meter and the qualities traditionally associated with it.

22. In addition to Jones's excellent book, see Edward D. Snyder, "Thomas Gray's Interest in Celtic," *Modern Philology,* 11 (1914):559–79, and the same author's *The Celtic Revival in English Literature* (Cambridge, Mass.: Harvard University Press, 1923).

23. Grierson, *The Background of English Literature* (London, Chatto and Windus, 1925), 210.

Chapter Six

1. Martin, *Essai,* 381.
2. Mason, *Memoirs,* 218.
3. Johnson, *Lives of the English Poets,* 3:425.
4. Jones, *Thomas Gray, Scholar,* 85.
5. Johnson, *Lives of the English Poets,* 3:441.
6. For an indication of his method of working, see his "Cambri" in Martin's *Chronologie,* esp. 175; the fullest discussion of his knowledge of Scandinavian is in G. L. Kittredge's "Appendix—Gray's Knowledge of Norse," in *Selections from the Poetry and Prose of Thomas Gray,* ed. William Lyon Phelps (Boston: Ginn, 1894), xli–l.
7. Richard Bridgman, "Weak Tocks: Coming to a Bad End in English Poetry of the Late Eighteenth Century," *Modern Philology* 80 (1983):278.
8. Cecil, "The Poetry of Thomas Gray," 249.
9. Gosse, *Gray,* 183; W. Elwin, review of Mitford's edition of Gray's correspondence, *Quarterly Review* 94 (December 1853):41; Martin, *Essai,* 388.
10. Mason, *Memoirs,* 116.
11. *Complete Poems* (89) uses Mason's text; Lonsdale, "with some misgivings," prints a later arrangement (*Poems,* 29).
12. Jones, *Thomas Gray, Scholar* 59.
13. Mason, *Memoirs,* 203.
14. Mason, *Memoirs,* 235.
15. Arthur Johnston, "Gray's 'The Triumphs of Owen,' " *Review of English Studies* 11 (1960):284–85.

Chapter Seven

1. Matthew Arnold, *Essays in Criticism,* 2d ser. (London: Macmillan, 1889), 91–92.
2. For a vigorous, learned denial of any such thing as "the Spirit of the Time" in literature, see George Boas, "In Search of the Age of Reason," in *Aspects of the Eighteenth Century,* ed. Earl R. Wasserman (Baltimore: Johns Hopkins University Press, 1965), 1–19.
3. W. K. Wimsatt, "Imitation as Freedom—1717–1798," *New Literary History* 1 (1970):217–18.
4. Quoted in F. O. Matthiessen, *American Renaissance* (New York: Oxford University Press, 1946), 133–34.
5. For a discussion of this viewpoint and its proponents see Morse Peckham, "Toward a Theory of Romanticism," *Publications of the Modern Language Association* 66 (1951):5–23.
6. Quoted in W. K. Wimsatt, Jr., *The Verbal Icon* (Lexington: University of Kentucky Press, 1954), 73.

7. Ricardo Quintana, *The Mind and Art of Jonathan Swift* (London: Oxford University Press, 1936), passim, esp. 65.

8. M. H. Abrams, *Natural Supernaturalism: Tradition and Revolution in Romantic Literature* (New York: Norton, 1971), 123.

9. Grierson, *Background of English Literature,* 203; Bertrand H. Bronson, "The Pre-Romantic or Post-Augustan Mode," *ELH: A Journal of English Literary History* 20 (1953):22.

10. On the visual in eighteenth-century English poetry, see, for example, Ralph Cohen, "The Augustan Mode in English Poetry," *Eighteenth-Century Studies* 1(1967):3–32; Josephine Miles, "A Change in the Language of Literature," *Eighteenth-Century Studies* 2 (1968):35–44; Rachel Trickett, "The Difficulties of Defining and Categorizing in the Augustan Period," *New Literary History* 1 (1970):163–79.

11. Morris Golden, *The Self Observed: Swift, Johnson, Wordsworth* (Baltimore: Johns Hopkins University Press, 1972), examines this idea.

12. Excellent essays examining Gray's impression on his contemporaries and on the later eighteenth and the nineteenth centuries are Roger Lonsdale, "Gray and Johnson: The Biographical Problem," and Alastair Macdonald, "Gray and his Critics: Patterns of Response in the Eighteenth and Nineteenth Centuries," in *Fearful Joy,* ed. Downey and Jones, 66–84, 172–97.

Selected Bibliography

PRIMARY SOURCES

Correspondence. Edited by Paget Toynbee and Leonard Whibley, with corrections and additions by H. W. Starr. 3 Vols. Oxford: Clarendon Press, 1971.

Designs by Mr. Bentley for Six Poems by Mr. T. Gray. London: Printed for R. Dodsley, in Pall-Mall, 1753.

Odes by Mr. Gray, Printed at Strawberry-Hill. London: R. & J. Dodsley in Pall-Mall, 1757.

Poems of Mr. Gray [and] *Memoirs of His Life and Writings,* by William Mason. York: A. Ward; London: J. Dodsley & J. Todd, 1775. *Memoirs* contains most of Gray's previously unpublished poetry, including the "Sonnet on the Death of Richard West," and a large number of Gray's letters (often in garbled texts).

Works. Edited by John Mitford. 5 vols. London: Wm. Pickering, 1835. Contains much material printed from Gray's notebooks and a number of letters more accurately printed than in Mason's *Memoirs.*

Works. Edited by Edmund Gosse. 4 vols. London: Macmillan, 1884. Some new prose from the notebooks.

An Elegy Written in a Country Church yard. Edited by Francis Griffin Stokes. Oxford: Clarendon Press, 1929. Contains a full discussion of the manuscripts of the poem and of the circumstances of its first publication.

An Elegy Wrote in a Country Church Yard [and] *The Eton College Manuscript.* Edited by George Sherburn. Los Angeles: Augustan Reprint Society, no. 31, 1951.

Complete Poems. Edited by H. W. Starr and J. R. Hendrickson. Oxford: Clarendon Press, 1966. The text cited in this study.

Selected Poems. Edited by Arthur Johnston. London: Edward Arnold, 1967. Prints both the Eton College manuscript and the standard version of the "Elegy."

Poems of Gray, Collins, and Goldsmith. Edited by Roger Lonsdale. London: Longmans, Green, 1969. Fully and authoritatively annotated.

SECONDARY SOURCES

Abrams, M. H. *The Mirror and the Lamp: Romantic Theory and the Critical Tradition.* 1953. Reprint. New York: Norton, 1958. Fundamental study of the imagination in the eighteenth and nineteenth centuries.

———*Natural Supernaturalism: Tradition and Revolution in Romantic Literature.* New York: Norton, 1971. Almost equally important.

The Age of Johnson; Essays Presented to Chauncey Brewster Tinker. New Haven: Yale University Press, 1949. Essays on a variety of writers of the mid-eighteenth century, including an interesting one on Gray by Donald M. Foerster.

Arnold, Matthew. "Thomas Gray." In *Essays in Criticism.* 2d ser. London: Macmillan, 1889, 69–99. A provocative essay by the great Victorian critic.

Bate, Walter J. *From Classic to Romantic.* Cambridge, Mass.: Harvard University Press, 1946. The intellectual background of the change in aesthetic taste at the end of the eighteenth century.

Bateson, F. W. *English Poetry: A Critical Introduction.* London: Longmans, Green, 1950. Includes a contentious essay on Gray.

Boswell, James. *Life of Johnson.* Edited by G. B. Hill; revised by L. F. Powell. 6 vols. Oxford: Clarendon Press, 1934. The best source of information about literary people and London life in the eighteenth century.

Bredvold, Louis I. "The Tendency Toward Platonism in Neo-Classical Esthetics." *ELH: A Journal of English Literary History* 1 (1934):91–119. Intellectual sources of a view shared by Gray.

Bronson, Bertrand H. "The Pre-Romantic or Post-Augustan Mode." *ELH: A Journal of English Literary History* 20 (1953):15–28. Surveys the aesthetic orientations of a variety of mid-eighteenth-century poets, including Gray.

Brooks, Cleanth. *The Well Wrought Urn: Studies in the Structure of Poetry.* New York: Reynal & Hitchcock, 1947. Includes an extended analysis of the "Elegy."

Brower, Reuben. *Alexander Pope: The Poetry of Allusion.* Oxford: Clarendon Press, 1959. Includes a thorough discussion of how Dryden and Pope used classical allusions, which is valid also for Gray.

Cecil, David. "The Poetry of Thomas Gray." In *Eighteenth Century English Literature,* edited by James L. Clifford. New York: Oxford University Press, 1959. An elegant appreciation.

———*Two Quiet Lives.* New York: Bobbs-Merrill, 1948. Pleasant, informed biographical study.

Camden, Carroll, ed. *Restoration and Eighteenth Century Literature.* Chicago: University of Chicago Press, 1963. Reprints significant essays.

Clifford, James L, ed. *Eighteenth Century English Literature: Modern Essays in Criticism.* New York: Oxford University Press, 1959. Reprints major essays from 1927 to 1959.

———, ed. *Man Versus Society in Eighteenth-Century Britain.* Cambridge: Cambridge University Press, 1968.

Cohen, Ralph. "The Augustan Mode in English Poetry." *Eighteenth-Century Studies* 1 (1967):3–32. A basic analysis of aesthetics and technique.

Coleridge, Samuel Taylor. *Biographia Literaria.* Edited by J. Shawcross. 2 vols. London: Oxford University Press, 1954. The literary theories of the most original and profound of English romantic critics.

Congreve, William. "A Discourse on the Pindaric Ode." *The Works of the English Poets,* edited by Alexander Chalmers. Vol. 10. London, 1810. This essay, originally printed in 1706, is considered the first in English to propose that Pindar's poetic structure be followed in English odes.

Crane, Ronald S. "Suggestions Toward a Genealogy of the 'Man of Feeling.' " *ELH: A Journal of English Literary History* 1 (1934):205–30. A basic source of information on the sentimentalism of Gray's day.

Doody, Margaret Anne. *The Daring Muse: Augustan Poetry Reconsidered.* Cambridge: Cambridge University Press, 1985. An exuberant, original, learned, and handsomely illustrated study.

Downey, James, and Jones, Ben, eds. *Fearful Joy: Papers from the Thomas Gray Bicentenary Conference at Carleton University.* Montreal: McGill-Queen's University Press, 1974. Original essays on Gray, many of very high quality.

Dyson, A.E. "The Ambivalence of Gray's Elegy." *Essays in Criticism* 7 (1957):257–61. A study of the language of the poem as it illuminates the psychological undercurrents and the social attitude in it.

Ellis, Frank H. "Gray's *Elegy:* The Biographical Problem in Literary Criticism." *Publications of the Modern Language Association* 66 (1951): 971–1008. Valuable analysis of structure and historical context.

Elton, Oliver. A *Survey of English Literature, 1730–1780.* 2 vols. London: Edward Arnold, 1928. Thorough, intelligent chapters on most of the significant figures of the time covered, including Gray.

Empson, William. *Some Versions of Pastoral.* London: Chatto & Windus, 1935. Includes a provocative discussion of the social attitudes in the "Elegy."

Fisher, J. "James Hammond and the Quatrain of Gray's *Elegy,*" *Modern Philology* 32 (1932):301–10. Hammond's importance as an innovator of the elegiac form.

Foladare, Joseph. "Gray's 'Frail Memorial' to West." *Publications of the*

Modern Language Association 75 (1960): 61–65. Milton's possible influence on the sonnet to West.

Golden, Morris. "A Decade's Bent: Names in the *Monthly Review* and the *Critical Review,* 1760–1769." *Bulletin of the New York Public Library* 79 (1976):336–61. An attempt to discover what was on people's minds.

———. "The Imagining Self in the Eighteenth Century." *Eighteenth Century Studies* 3 (1969):4–27. An examination of a literary stance.

———. *The Self-Observed: Swift, Johnson, Wordsworth.* Baltimore: Johns Hopkins University Press, 1972. Relations between observing and acting selves in literature.

Goldsmith, Oliver. *Collected Works.* Edited by Arthur Friedman. 5 vols. Oxford: Clarendon Press, 1966. Contains various references and allusions to Gray as well as Goldsmith's review of the *Odes* in volume 1.

Gosse, Edmund W. *Gray.* English Men of Letters Series. New York: Harper, 1882. Gracefully written, critically intelligent, and biographically untrustworthy.

Grierson, H. J. C. *The Background of English Literature.* London: Chatto & Windus, 1925. Contains a wise essay on Gray and Blake.

Griffin, M. H. "Thomas Gray, Classical Augustan." *Classical Journal* 36 (1941):473–82. Discusses Gray's Latin poems.

Hagstrum, Jean H. *The Sister Arts: The Tradition of Literary Pictorialism and English Poetry from Dryden to Gray.* Chicago: University of Chicago Press, 1958. Useful on poetic technique of the period and essential for an understanding of Gray's Pindaric Odes.

Johnson, Samuel. *Lives of the English Poets.* Edited by G. B. Hill. 3 vols. Oxford: Clarendon Press, 1905. Includes the short, devastating study that is the beginning of Gray criticism.

Johnston, Arthur. "Gray's 'The Triumphs of Owen.' " *Review of English Studies* 11 (1960):275–85. Gray's limited knowledge of Welsh and his success as an imitator of the original.

Jones, W. Powell. "The Contemporary Reception of Gray's *Odes.*" *Modern Philology* 28 (1930):61–82. Discussion of the sale and critical response to the poems.

———. "Johnson and Gray: A Study in Literary Antagonism." *Modern Philology* 56 (1959):243–53. The attacks on Johnson's "Life of Gray," and the characters of the two writers.

———. 'Mute Inglorious Gray." *Emory University Quarterly* 11 (1955):199–207. Gray's personality, illuminated by some new material from his notebooks.

———. "Thomas Gray's Library." *Modern Philology* 35 (1938):257–78. Mainly a list of books that Gray bought from 1760 on.

———. *Thomas Gray, Scholar: The True Tragedy of an Eighteenth-Century*

Gentleman. Cambridge, Harvard University Press, 1937. An invaluable study of Gray's reading and his notebooks.

———. "The Vogue of Natural History in England, 1750–1770." *Annals of Science* 2 (1937):345–52. The background of Gray's studies of botany and insect biology.

Ketton-Cremer, R. W. *Thomas Gray.* Cambridge: Cambridge University Press, 1955. The best biography in English thus far.

Kittredge, G. L. "Appendix—Gray's Knowledge of Norse." In *Selections from the Poetry and Prose of Thomas Gray,* edited by W. L. Phelps. Boston: Ginn, 1894.

Kliger, Samuel. *The Goths in England: A Study in Seventeenth and Eighteenth Century Thought.* Cambridge, Mass.: Harvard University Press, 1952. The idea of the "Gothic" in politics, religion, and literature.

Lipking, Lawrence. "Quick Poetic Eyes: Another look at Literary Pictorialism." In *Articulate Images: The Sister Arts from Hogarth to Tennyson,* edited by Richard Wendorf, 3–25. Minneapolis: University of Minnesota Press, 1983. Perceptive on the "Elegy."

Lovejoy, Arthur O. *Essays in the History of Ideas.* Baltimore: Johns Hopkins University Press, 1948. Contains authoritative studies on the intellectual background of the eighteenth century, particularly " 'Nature' as Aesthetic Norm" (69–77) and "The Parallel of Deism and Classicism" (78–98).

———. *The Great Chain of Being.* Cambridge, Mass.: Harvard University Press, 1936. The standard work on a major philosophical concept prevalent through the eighteenth century.

Maclean, Norman. "From Action to Image: Theories of the Lyric in the Eighteenth Century." In *Critics and Criticism,* edited by R. S. Crane. 408–60. Chicago: University of Chicago Press, 1952. The history and nature of the ode in the period.

Martin, Roger. *Chronologie de la vie et de l'cœuvre de Thomas Gray.* Paris: Presses Universitaires de France, 1931. Includes, besides the discussion of chronology, material from Gray's notebooks never before printed.

———. *Essai sur Thomas Gray.* London: Oxford University Press, 1935. The best biographical and critical study of Gray.

McKenzie, Alan T. *Thomas Gray. A Reference Guide.* Boston: G. K. Hall, 1982. A valuable compendium of secondary sources on Gray.

Micklus, Robert. "Voices in the Wind: The Eton Ode's Ambivalent Prospect of Maturity." *English Langauge Notes* 18 (1981):181–86. The poem as contrast of fancy and reality.

Miles, Josephine. "A Change in the Language of Literature." *Eighteenth Century Studies* 2 (1968):35–44. Valuable on the grammar of poetry in the eighteenth century.

Monk, Samuel H. *The Sublime.* New York: Modern Language Association,

1935. Historical study of the idea of the sublime in eighteenth-century aesthetics.

Northup, C. S. *Bibliography of Thomas Gray.* New Haven: Yale University Press, 1917. An authoritative listing of Gray's writings, their editions, and critical comment on them.

Osgood, C. G. "Lady Phillipina Knight and Her Boswell." *Princeton University Library Chronicle* 4 (1943):37–49. Includes an anecdote about Gray.

Pattison, Robert. "Gray's 'Ode on the Death of a Favourite Cat': A Rationalist's Aesthetic." *University of Toronto Quarterly* 49 (1979–80): 156–64. Selima as the Lockean mind.

Paulson, Ronald. *Popular and Polite Art in the Age of Hogarth and Fielding.* South Bend: University of Notre Dame Press, 1979. Excellent analysis of the context for Gray's poetry.

Peckham, Morse. "Toward a Theory of Romanticism." *Publications of the Modern Language Association* 66 (1951):5–23. Thoughtful, stimulating discussion of the changing intellectual attitudes of the late eighteenth century.

Pindar, *Odes.* Translated by Richmond Lattimore. Chicago: University of Chicago Press, 1941. A widely admired translation of the poems that Gray used as models for his Pindaric Odes of 1757.

Reed, Amy Louise. *The Background of Gray's Elegy: A Study in the Taste for Melancholy Poetry 1700–1751.* New York: Columbia University Press, 1924. Outdated in places, but still valuable.

Shenstone, William. *Works.* 2 vols. London: R. & J. Dodsley, 1764. Contains a basic discussion of the elegy form by a leading practitioner as well as the poems that, in manuscript, might have influenced Gray's poem.

Shepard, Odell. "A Youth to Fortune and to Fame Unknown." *Modern Philology* 20 (1923):347–73. Advances the untenable, though seminal, theory that Richard West is the subject of the "Epitaph" to Gray's "Elegy.'

Sherburn, George. "The Restoration and Eighteenth Century." In *A Literary History of England*, edited by Albert C. Baugh. New York: Appleton-Century-Crofts, 1948. Reprinted, 1967, with updated bibliographies by R. P. Bond. A standard work.

Shuster, George N. *The English Ode from Milton to Keats.* New York: Columbia University Press, 1940. Though critically valueless, still a useful history of the form.

Snyder, Edward D. *The Celtic Revival in English Literature.* Cambridge, Mass.: Harvard University Press, 1923. The standard work on an important intellectual and literary phenomenon of the time.

———. "Thomas Gray's Interest in Celtic." *Modern Philology* 11

(1914):559–79. The best study of Gray's use of Welsh verse forms in his imitations and in "The Bard."

Starr, Herbert W. *Bibliography of Thomas Gray 1917–1951.* Philadelphia: University of Pennsylvania, 1953. A useful supplement and continuation of Northup.

———. *Gray as a Literary Critic.* Philadelphia: University of Pennsylvania Press, 1941. The only study of the subject, based primarily on Gray's correspondence.

———. " 'A Youth to Fortune and to Fame Unknown': A Re-Estimation." *Journal of English and Germanic Philology* 48 (1949). The subject of the epitaph is "merely a young rustic versifier, a poetic ideal of a sort."

———, ed. *Twentieth Century Interpretations of Gray's Elegy.* Englewood Cliffs, N. J.: Prentice-Hall, 1968. Fine introduction and a collection of major essays covering the variety of approaches to that date.

Sullivan, Alvin, ed. *British Literary Magazines: The Augustan Age and the Age of Johnson, 1698–1788.* Westport, Conn.: Greenwood, 1983. Brief individual essays on the major periodicals with literary associations.

Sutherland, John H. "The Stonecutter in Gray's 'Elegy.' " *Modern Philology* 55 (1957):11–13. Rather than a stonecutter, there is a fictional narrator who is also the subject of the Epitaph.

Swearingen, James E. "Wordsworth on Gray." *Studies in English Literature* 14 (1974):489–509. Valuable on the aesthetic positions of the two poets, useful analysis of the Sonnet to West.

Swedenberg, H. T., Jr. "Thomas Gray's 'Journal for 1754 from the first of March.' " *Huntington Library Quarterly* 3 (1939):77–102. Prints the journal for the first time.

Tovey, Duncan C. *Gray and His Friends.* Cambridge: Cambridge University Press, 1890. Includes Gray material from the notebooks not before printed.

Trickett, Rachel. "The Difficulties of Defining and Categorizing in the Augustan Period." *New Literary History* 1 (1970):163–79. Learned especially on technique and aesthetic theories.

Van Houk, La Rue. "New Light on the Classical Scholarship of Thomas Gray." *American Journal of Philology* 57 (1936):1–9. Discusses Gray's classical studies and classical influences on his poems.

Walpole, Horace. *Correspondence.* Vols. 13–14. Edited by W. S. Lewis, George L. Lam, and Charles H. Bennett. New Haven: Yale University Press, 1948. Walpole-Gray correspondence, in some details adding to the Toynbee-Whibley edition of Gray's *Correspondence.* The immense edition of all of Walpole's correspondence contains a great many references to Gray.

Wasserman, Earl R. "The Inherent Values of 18th Century Personification." *Publications of the Modern Language Association* 65 (1950):435–63. Neoclassical theories justifying a technique important in Gray's poetry.

———, ed. *Aspects of the Eighteenth Century.* Baltimore: Johns Hopkins University Press, 1965. Reprints some fundamental essays.

Whibley, Leonard. "The Foreign Tour of Gray and Walpole." *Blackwood's Magazine* 227 (1930):813–27. A survey of the trip and a discussion of the probable cause of the quarrel.

———. "Thomas Gray at Eton." *Blackwood's Magazine* 225 (1929):611–23. Character of Gray's father, conditions at Eton in Gray's time.

———. "Thomas Gray, Undergraduate." *Blackwood's Magazine* 227 (1930):273–86. Cambridge's low state during the eighteenth century.

Williams, Kathleen, ed. *Backgrounds to Eighteenth-Century Literature.* Scranton: Chandler, 1971. Reprints a variety of major essays.

Wimsatt, W. K. "Imitation as Freedom—1717–1798." *New Literary History* 1 (1970):215–36. Wise discussion of an issue important to Gray.

Wordsworth, William. Preface. *Lyrical Ballads.* 2d ed. In *Poetical Works.* Vol. 2, Edited by E. de Selincourt. Oxford: Clarendon Press, 1944. Includes the famous attack on Gray's diction.

Index

Abrams, M. H., 123–24
Addison, Joseph, 124
Aeschylus, 98
Agrippina (mother of Nero), 102–5
Akenside, Mark, 15
Algarotti, Francesco, 24
Aneurin (a Welsh bard), 112
Anstey, Christopher, 55
Arabian Nights, 125
Aristotle, 20, 24
Armstrong, John, 15
Arnold, Matthew, 115–16, 126, 132
Arthur, King, 84
Ashton, Thomas, 7
Augustus, 76
Austen, Jane, 95, 118, 123

Baif, Jean Antoine de, 38n11
Bailey, Margery, 57n8
Bartholin, 95, 97
Bate, Walter J., 20n4
Bateson, F.W., 59n13
"Battle of Brunanburh," 96
"Battle of Maldon," 96
Beattie, James, 93, 100; "The Minstrel," 25, 28, 86
Bedingfield, Edward, 12, 13, 70
Bentley, Richard, 42, 44n18, 46–48, 52–53, 61, 64–65, 93, 107–9
Berkeley, Bishop George, 123
Blake, William, 45, 118, 120, 121, 122, 123, 124, 126, 128, 132
Bloomfield, Morton A., 31n15
Boas, George, 118n2
Boileau, Nicolas, 21
Bonstetten, Charles Victor de, 12
Boswell, James, 5, 6, 16, 121
Bridgman, Richard, 98
British Magazine, 58
Bronson, Bertrand, 21, 127
Brontë, Emily, *Wuthering Heights,* 126
Brooks, Cleanth, 36, 58, 60–61, 62, 66, 67
Browning, Robert, "My Last Duchess," 2
Burns, Robert, 130
Byron, George Gordon Noel, Lord, 123, 131, 132; *Childe Harold's Pilgrimage,* 132

Cadwallo (a Welsh bard), 92
Caesar, Julius, 83
Camus, Albert, 63
Carlyle, Thomas, 121, 123
Carte, Thomas, 80
Cecil, David, 51, 99
Charles II, 76
Chatterton, Thomas, 94
Churchill, Charles, 94, 99, 112
Chute, John, 10
Cibber, Colley, 14
Claude (Claude Lorrain), 72
Clerke, Jane, 113
Cobham, Lady Anne, 90–94
Cohen, Ralph, 130n10
Coleridge, Samuel Taylor, 43, 100, 116, 120–21, 123, 124, 130; Kubla Khan," 117, 126
Collins, William, 34, 35n7, 70, 95, 125, 131; "Ode to Fear," 41
Congreve, William, 69–70
Court Magazine, 15n17
Cowley, Abraham, 34, 69, 75
Cowper, William, 26
Critical Review, 51, 71

Dante Alighieri, 76, 77
Defoe, Daniel, 94; *Moll Flanders,* 124
Denham, John, "Cooper's Hill," 125
Dilworth, Ernest, 38n11
Dixon, Richard Watson, 39
Dodsley, Robert, 13, 26, 59, 93, 107
Donne, John, 100
Doody, Margaret Anne, 31n15, 44n18, 64
Downey, James, 62n23
Dryden, John, 1, 14, 44, 74–75, 76, 81, 100, 109, 119, 120, 122, 128; "Alexander's Feast," 52, 69; "To the Pious Memory of the Acomplisht Young Lady Mrs. Anne Killigrew"; "Religio Laici," 106, 108; "To Sir Godfrey Kneller," 108; "A Song for St. Cecilia's Day," 75
Dyson, A.E., 62n19

Ecclesiastes, 56
Edward I, 80–88, 91, 97, 128

Edward III, 83
Ehrenpreis, Irvin, 82n18
Eliot, T.S., 115, 125
Elizabeth I, 76, 84, 93
Elliott, Roger, 58n12
Ellis, Frank H., 44n18, 61–62, 66
Elton, Oliver, 36, 44, 46, 51–52, 57
Elwin, W., 59n13, 100
Empson, William, 58–59
Epicurus, 25
Etough, Henry, 113
Ezekiel (the prophet), 82

Faulkner, William, 45
Fielding, Henry, 95, 117, 120, 124; *Jonathan Wild,* 33; *Joseph Andrews,* 33; *Tom Jones,* 116, 122, 124
Fisher, J., 57n9
Fitzgerald, F. Scott, 45
Franklin, Benjamin, 119
Freud, Sigmund, 92, 117

Garrick, David, 71
Garrick, Eva Maria, 73
Gay, John, 124, 125
George II, 14
Gibbon, Edward, 16, 107
Gilmore, Thomas B., Jr., 44n18
Gloucester, Gilbet de Clare, Earl of, 81
Glover, Richard, 15
Golden, Morris, 15n17, 17n19, 130n11
Goldsmith, Oliver, 26, 35n7, 71–72, 94, 115–16; *Citizen of the World,* 122; *Deserted Village,* 18, 45, 125, 126; *Traveller,* 18, 74, 106, 107; *Vicar of Wakefield,* 116
Gosse, Edmund, 22n8, 41, 49n19, 54, 100, 107, 129
Grafton, Augustus Henry Fitzroy, 3rd duke of, 100–2
Gray, Dorothy (Thomas Gray's mother), 3, 5, 32, 79, 88, 91, 103–4
Gray, Philip (Thomas Gray's father), 3, 32, 88
Gray, Thomas:

Correspondence, 3n3, 5n7, 5n8, 7, 8, 9, 10, 11, 12, 13, 14, 15, 18n1, 19, 21, 22, 23, 24, 25, 26, 27, 28, 29, 30–31, 32, 46, 55, 55n2, 70, 71, 73, 80, 90, 91, 100, 103, 105, 107

WORKS:
"Agrippina, A Tragedy," 83, 102–5, 114
Alcaic Ode, 33
"The Alliance of Education and Government," 15, 18, 25, 59, 105–7, 111, 114
"The Bard," 3, 16, 22, 23, 24, 41, 79–89, 92, 94, 96, 97, 100, 101, 102, 104, 105, 106, 107, 108, 110, 115, 125, 128, 130, 131, 132
Ad C: Favonium Aristium, 32
"Cambri," 80, 95
"The Candidate," 112
"Caradoc," 112
"Conan," 112
"De Principiis Cogitandi," 18, 25, 38, 111, 114, 128
"The Descent of Odin," 27, 97–98
"The Death of Hoel," 112
"Elegy Written in a Country Church-Yard," 1, 2, 3, 12, 13, 15, 18, 22, 27, 34, 35, 36, 41, 42, 43, 49, 50, 52, 54–68, 79, 80, 82, 83, 86, 87, 88, 91, 92, 97, 101, 102, 105, 106, 107, 108, 110, 113, 114, 115, 127, 128, 129, 130, 131, 133
Epitaphs, 113
"The Fatal Sisters," 27, 95–97, 98
"Hymn to Ignorance," 105
"Lines Spoken by the Ghost of John Dennis," 113
"A Long Story," 13, 26, 90–94, 101, 105, 113
"The Measures of Verse," 30
"Metrum: Observations on English Metre. . . .," 29–30
Norse and Celtic imitations, 13, 27, 94–99, 129
"Ode to Adversity," 34, 41–44, 48, 49, 52, 87, 129, 132
"Ode on the Death of a Favourite Cat, Drowned in a Tub of Gold Fishes," 50–53, 119
"Ode on a Distant Prospect of Eton College," 12, 34, 42, 43, 44–50, 52, 67, 73, 78, 83, 87, 97, 102, 105, 110, 123, 128, 129, 130
"Ode for Music," 59, 100–2, 105, 106
"Ode on the Pleasure Arising from Vicissitude," 4n6, 34, 109–11, 114, 132
"Ode on the Spring," 33, 34–37, 42, 44, 45, 63, 67, 68, 83, 87, 92, 104, 110, 129
"On Lord Holland's Seat near Margate, Kent," 99

Poems (1768), 27, 59, 93, 94
Pindaric Odes (*Odes*, 1757), 1, 3, 15, 18, 23, 26, 52, 69–89, 102, 110, 127, 128, 129, 130, 131, 133
"The Progress of Poesy," 1, 3, 10, 13, 23, 69, 72–79, 80, 82, 88, 100, 101, 107, 108, 109, 114, 116, 128
"Satire on the Heads of Houses," 113
Six Poems (1753), 13, 59, 107
"Sketch of His Own Character," 111–12
"Songs," 113
"Sonnet on the Death of Richard West," 34, 37–41, 44, 99, 114, 128
"Stanzas to Mr. Bentley," 107–9, 110, 113, 116
"Tophet," 113
"The Triumphs of Owen," 27, 98
Welsh translations, 112
"William Shakespeare to Mrs. Anne," 113

Grierson, H.J.C., 89, 127
Gwalchmai, 98

Hagstrum, Jean, 12n5, 72, 75, 77, 82, 85
Hammond, James, 57
Hampden, John, 67
Hardy, Thomas, 132–33
Hatton, Christopher, 93
Hawkesworth, John, 15
Hemingway, Ernest, 45
Hendrickson, J.R., 33n1
Henry V, 84
Henry VI, 84
Henry VII, 84
Hoel (a Welsh Bard), 92
Holland, Henry Fox, Lord, 99
Homer, 19
Hopkins, Gerard Manley, 39
Horace, 19, 41, 56, 57, 76, 120, 131
How, William Taylor, 24
Hume, David, 15
Hurd, Richard, 9
Hutchings, W., 62n23
Hygden, Ranulf, 82

Isabel of France (Edward II's queen), 83
Isocrates, 106,

James II, 76
Job, 56
Johnson, Samuel, 6, 15, 24, 25, 26, 87, 117, 119, 120, 123, 129; "Life of Gray," 6, 31, 34–35, 41–42, 44, 50, 51–52, 55, 69, 72, 76, 81, 86, 93–94, 95; "Life of Pope," 113; *Rambler*, 124; *Rasselas*, 121, 125, 130; *Vanity of Human Wishes*, 107, 116, 130
Johnston, Arthur, 88n21, 112n15
Jones, Ben, 62n23
Jones, W. Powell, 4n6, 16n18, 19n2, 38n10, 69, 70, 80, 88, 94, 100, 106, 131
Jonson, Ben, 34
Juvenal, 19, 120

Keats, John, 34, 40, 121, 123, 131, 132
Ketton-Cremer, R.W., 2–3, 34
King, Edward, 61
Kittredge, G.L., 95n6
Kliger, Samuel, 21
Knight, Lady Phillipina, 4

Landor, Walter Savage, 38n11
Langhorne, John, 4n6, 27
Lawrence, D.H., 118, 120
Lee, Nathaniel, 103
Lipking, Lawrence, 66
Literary Magazine, 71
Lloyd, Robert, 55
Locke, John, 18, 51, 122
Longinus, 20, 71
Lonsdale, Roger, 35n7, 38n11, 42, 55n2, 57, 59, 74n12, 88, 103n11, 133n12
Louis XIV, 76
Lucretius, 25, 56
Lyles, Albert M., 44n18

Macdonald, Alastair, 133n12
Maclean, Norman, 41
Macpherson, James, 21, 26, 27, 94
Magazine of Magazines, 13
Margaret of Anjou (Henry VI's queen), 102
Martial, 56
Martin, Roger, 3, 16, 17, 33, 35, 51, 87, 91, 98, 100, 130
Mason, Mary, 113
Mason, William, 4n6, 5, 6, 10, 15, 16, 23, 25, 28, 29, 34, 54–55, 57, 59, 63, 75, 80, 92, 103, 106, 108, 109, 113
Melville, Herman, *Moby Dick*, 123
Merlin, 84
Micklus, Robert, 44n18
Miles, Josephine, 130n10
Miller, Phillip, 10
Milton, John, 1, 2, 20, 30, 34n3, 41, 74, 76, 77, 78, 79, 97, 101, 109, 127, 128;

Comus, 100; "Il Penseroso," 43, 56, 101; "L'Allegro," 43, 78; "Lycidas," 61–62; "On the Morning of Christ's Nativity," 74, 101; *Paradise Lost,* 73, 74, 85, 105
Mitford, John, 59n13, 73, 100
Monk, Samuel H., 21n5
Montesquieu, Charles Louis de Secondat, 106
Monthly Review, 27n12, 71–72
Moore, Judith K., 38n11
Mortimer, Edmund de, 81, 87

Nangle, Benjamin Christie, 29n12
Nero, 103–5
Newton, Isaac, 51, 101, 119
Nicholls, Norton, 6, 12, 18, 87, 107

O'Casey, Sean, 133
Osgood, C.G., 4
Ossian (a Gaelic bard), 26, 27

Parry, John, 80
Pater, Walter, 123
Pattison, Robert, 51
Peckham, Morse, 62n23, 121n5
Percy, Bishop Thomas, 94
Petrarch (Francesco Petrarca), 38n11, 40
Pindar, 19, 34, 69–89, 127, 130
Plato, 14, 18, 59, 77, 88, 101, 128
Pope, Alexander, 20, 24, 26, 27, 99, 106, 109, 119, 120, 122, 130; *Dunciad,* 33, 105; Epistle to Dr. Arbuthnot," 124; "Epistle to Mr. Jervas," 108; "Essay on Criticism," 18, 19, 20, 74, 107; *Essay on Man,* 26, 73, 118, 124; *Rape of the Lock,* 51, 67, 124, 125; "Windsor Forest," 125
Psalms, 56

Quintana, Ricardo, 123

Racine, Jean, 76
Raphael, 82
Reed, Amy Louise, 55–56
Reynolds, Joshua, 121
Richard II, 83
Richard III, 83, 84
Richardson, Samuel, 94, 116, 117; *Clarissa,* 124
Roberts, William Hayward, 55
Rogers, Ann (Thomas Gray's aunt), 91
Rogers, Jonathan (Thomas Gray's uncle), 21
Rosa, Salvator, 72
Rousseau, Jean Jacques, 118, 124, 132

Sandwich, John Montagu, 4th earl of, 112
Sarto, Andrea del, 23
Schaub, Lady, 90–94
Seneca, 18, 56
Shaftesbury, Anthony Ashley Cooper, 3rd earl of, 18, 122
Shakespeare, William, 1, 28, 40, 74, 76, 77, 81, 85, 109, 127, 128; sonnets, 1
Shelley, Percy Bysshe, 110, 121, 124, 126, 130, 132; *Adonais,* 131; "Hymn to Intellectual Beauty," 123; *Prometheus Unbound,* 132; "To a Skylark," 132
Shenstone, William, 56, 56n7
Shepard, Odell, 61
Sherburn, George, 59n13
Sheridan, Thomas, 15
Shuster, George N., 34
Sidney, Sir Philip, 40
Smart, Christopher, 4
Smollett, Tobias George, 94
Snyder, Edward D., 88n22
Song of Deborah, 98
Spacks, Patricia Meyer, 38n11
Speed, Henrietta, 90–94, 113
Spenser, Edmund, 1, 20, 40, 44, 100; *Faerie Queene,* 85
Squire, Samuel, 111
Starr, Herbert W., 25n11, 33n1, 56n7, 61n18, n19, 62n23
Steele, James, 80n14
Steele, Richard, 124
Stephen, Leslie, 5
Sterne, Laurence, 94; *Sentimental Journal,* 22; *Tristram Shandy,* 106, 116, 130
Stonhewer, Richard, 18n1
Stuart, Charles Edward ("Bonnie Prince Charlie"), 57
Stuart, James Francis Edward, 57
Sutherland, John H., 62n23
Swearingen, James E., 39n12
Swedenberg, H.T., Jr., 19n2
Swift, Jonathan, 10, 26, 69, 94, 99, 120, 122, 123, 125, 130; "The Author upon Himself," 92; *Battle of the Books,* 20; *Gulliver's Travels,* 118, 119, 123, 124; "A Modest Proposal," 125; *Tale of a Tub,* 118, 119, 123

Taliessin (a Welsh bard), 84
Tayler, Irene, 64
Temple, William, 5
Tennyson, Alfred, 132
Theocritus, 61, 119

Thomson, James, 119, 125; *Castle of Indolence,* 124; *Liberty,* 18, 74; *Seasons,* 125; *Winter,* 107
Tibullus, 57
Torfaeus, Thormodus, 95
Tovey, Duncan C., 23n9
Townshend, Charles, 111
Toynbee, Paget, 3n3
Trickett, Rachel, 130n10

Urien (a Welsh bard), 92

Virgil, 56, 57, 76, 119
Viry, Joseph Marie de, 90
Voltaire, Francois Marie Arouet de, 5, 18

Wagner, Richard, 97
Walpole, Horace, 6, 7, 8, 13, 21, 26, 32, 42, 46–48, 50, 52, 54– 55, 59, 61, 93, 103
Walpole, Sir Robert, 33
Warton, Thomas, 15
Wasserman, Earl R., 31n15, 42
Watson, George, 62n23
Weinbrot, Howard D., 58n12, 80n12
West, Richard, 7, 8, 9, 11, 19, 25, 30, 33, 37–41, 54–55, 57, 61, 88, 105, 114, 129
Wharton, Robin, 113
Wharton, Thomas, 80, 113
Whibley, Leonard, 3n3, 4n6
Whitman, Walt, 118, 120, 132
Williams, Sir William, 113
Wimsatt, W.K., 19–20
Wordsworth, William, 42, 116, 120, 121, 124, 129, 130, 131, 132; "Lines Composed a Few Miles above Tintern Abbey," 123; *Lyrical Ballads,* Preface, 31, 37–40, 49, 97; "Ode to Duty," 132; *Prelude,* 124, 131

Yeats, William Butler, 132
Young, Edward, 15; *Night Thoughts,* 56–57, 124